THE
LANDLORD'S
SURVIVAL
GUIDE

THE TRULY PRACTICAL INSIDER HANDBOOK
FOR ALL PRIVATE LANDLORDS

LESLEY HENDERSON

howtobooks

Published by How To Books Ltd,
Spring Hill House, Spring Hill Road,
Begbroke, Oxford OX5 1RX. United Kingdom.
Tel: (01865) 375794. Fax: (01865) 379162.
info@howtobooks.co.uk
www.howtobooks.co.uk

British Library Cataloguing in Publication Data
A catalogue record for this book is available from the British Library

ISBN 978 1 84528 224 0

Cover design by Baseline Arts Ltd, Oxford
Produced for How To Books by Deer Park Productions, Tavistock, Devon
Typeset by PDQ Typesetting, Newcastle-under-Lyme, Staffs.
Printed and bound by Bell & Bain Ltd, Glasgow

Contents

Preface

What a *difference* a decade can make!

Who could possibly have guessed that a single word could revolutionise an entire industry? A few fanatics might even claim that Europe too has felt the force of this change as British property wealth has fuelled price growth right across the continent.

And this magical word? *Shorthold*.

Some well-documented events took place in the 1980s, for example, the relaxation of finance regulation including lending on housing; a revolution in the availability of credit; new, 'flexible' workforce demands; massive council house sales; plus the 1988 Housing Acts, which contained the shorthold option meant for a few new tenancies. Together, these alterations changed the entire UK lending climate. Caution had 'gone with the wind'. Borrowing was the new buzzword.

With the benefit of hindsight, the addition of the word 'shorthold' to an obscure Housing Act opened floodgates of money, which had, for almost 20 years, been firmly locked shut on my industry. The older ethic of creating wealth before buying something has become as obsolete as horse drawn carts. These days we borrow to consume on virtually *everything* – on an unprecedented scale. Cars. Holidays. And, most importantly of all – property.

Until only a decade ago, investing in property that you couldn't get back, unless your low rent tenant *let* you have it back, was simply bad business. Lenders wouldn't touch it with poles. So adding 'shorthold' to the 1988 legislation (which actually intended to create *slightly* more landlord-friendly rentals, market rents and reduced paperwork) was absolute *dynamite*.

The 1988 legislation intent on creating assured tenancies was swept sideways as lenders queued up to loan money to investors willing to give their tenants assured shorthold leases with virtually no security of tenure beyond a few temporary rights. Risk had been reduced. Investment could begin. And by golly, have we all partied.

The Buy to Let (BLT) phenomena has fuelled equity release and investment on an unparalleled scale. All of which was expertly exploited by the only people quick enough off the block. ARLA (Association of Residential Letting Agents) understood the real significance of these simple shortholds and ARLA *pounced!* And in fairness, for that at least, every modern landlord owes it a debt of gratitude.

In theory, the whole BTL concept is *exceedingly simple.* Borrow to buy. Tenants pay off the borrowings. Landlord gets the building for free. At least that's the promised dream. Reality and dreams rarely make great pals. Here, they're barely on speaking terms. The truth is, having cranked up property prices by buying anything with rental potential, we, as landlords have collectively disengaged 'profit' from effort. At today's prices, the profit is strictly long term. And the biggest irony of all? Many new landlords with the highest lending exposures don't even get a taste of their profit. In today's climate, investors taking *all the risk* usually make fewer profits by a stretch than agents who take none.

Full management always was and still is a 'top end product' – not an essential. A bit like paying a chauffeur sooner than learning how to drive.

But in a skilful manipulation of both media and marketplace, the lettings industry has insisted that letting is 'complicated' and that landlords need a new breed of 'experts'. So, ask yourself three simple questions.

- *Why?* When the 1988 Housing Act had created such easy to set up and terminate tenancies?
- *Where?* had all these experienced agents come from in the space of a year or so?
- *Why?* would landlords need them now, when the rules had just been designed to make life so easy?

What's even more worrying is quality and financial control of agents. You can obtain a Degree in Knitting Design, but this government has shown no interest in creating a meaningful, independently validated qualification for the multi-billion pound lettings industry; let alone a financial overseer with teeth, like the ones your building society, pensions advisor or even your home insurers *have* to provide.

So, your letting agent may be okay, or may be an absolute donkey. He has no qualifications or diplomas to hang on his wall but those of his own trade organisation. Genuine professions take years of study – not a few hours 'training' at a hotel seminar. Training, which if you look at it closely enough, you'll find concentrates in selling more and more commission generating products and services. It's a hard truth to recognise, but that charming double-breasted smile may really *be* experienced, but it *could* have been selling wet fish last week.

Try remembering that landlords take 100 per cent of the risk. Agents survive by taking a hefty slab of *your risk*.

One final hard truth. Using 'yields' to cover interest on vast lending is an entirely new concept. It's a uniquely UK solution to a uniquely UK situation. BTL landlords are financial guinea pigs: testing an untried idea and lacking the kind of advice that they really need. That's the real risk that Buy to Let investors face. In reality, property remains a game of risk and don't let anyone tell you otherwise. Property prices have tripled in the last ten years – but any investment can contract as fast as it boomed. As landlords, you'll have little influence on the overall performance of the UK economy, which drives property prices and – as such – all you can do is minimise your own exposure to your own unique set of risks. Knowledge is the only way to reduce risk in such an expensive game of chance. Margins for error in the lettings game are narrowing all the time. Profitability is now tight. And borrowing to buy can be a tricky enough equation without handing over the difference between profit and loss every month in astronomical fees because you don't feel you know enough to have any option but to use agents.

Agency fees can make the real difference between a healthy, profitable investment ... or an albatross.

Introduction

How the guide works

Learning things can be dull. It can also take too long. And, let's be honest, most landlords don't have that kind of time because they're out earning money in demanding day jobs.

So, I asked myself, how could a new or potential landlord get to grips with the numerous simple steps involved with successful rentals – without hours of hard slog? How could I update the majority of landlords about massive new regulations which came into force in April 2006 and early 2007 on Houses in Multiple Occupation and *compulsory* Tenant Deposit Schemes, which will affect every new tenancy?

How could I provide 'enough' information to ensure that landlords can check what their agency is up to? And convince readers that letting property is *not* as time consuming or risky as you've been led to believe! A nuts and bolts guide that provided exactly that was needed.

So, *this* guide needed to be useful, detailed, concise, comprehensive and most importantly contain instructions, which could be easily replicated by amateur landlords. Something that was equally useful for the established landlord encountering a single problem - needing to learn about new legislation or having agency problems – right through to complete novices.

How could I provide access to all those 'elusive' little details that everyone else in the letting business is so anxious to keep to themselves?

To achieve this, I divided information into lessons. Each lesson is jam packed with detail and insider tips.

Most lessons will only take minutes to read (although a few earlier ones take a little more (well spent) time.

Each lesson tells you exactly what you need to do for the best results and *why*. Because *none* of this takes long – *none* of it is tricky – and none of it *needs* agents.

The lessons include:

- Not just 'valuations' but exactly how to do your own and why you need to learn how to do this *long before* you ever begin buying buildings.

- Not just 'leases' but *what* and *why* they are *what* they are, *where* to get hold of them, plus of course, *how* to fill them in and enforce them.

Each lesson has tips, tenant management skills, time management ideas, and problem solving advice, stacks of *free, reliable* information and guidance to support you, plus responsible, helpful websites and phone numbers.

And, because the *Daily Telegraph*'s reviewer of my *Tenant's Survival Guide* liked them so much, I've included more toe curling anecdotes to make you grin or grimace! Unlike much of what's written on this topic, all my anecdotes are true.

The *Guide* is a 'pick and mix' concept. If you've never invested before, you'll *need* to read everything. If you're just problem solving, skip to the relevant topic using the index.

Anyone can make paper profits in a bullish property market – being well enough informed to handle those grisly bear type markets is what separates success from failure in the letting's game.

However, if you're looking for a bit of straight talking about what is a massive investment or if you're simply interested enough to learn and want to increase your own bottom line rather than some agent's ... then this is the guide for you.

And finally, for those of you who find this whole topic absolutely fascinating please read the Preface, where I blow off a little steam!

Author's note: In order to produce an uncompromising 'warts and all' guide, this publication has accepted no advertising or endorsements of any kind.

Lesson 1

Learning the ropes when buying property

As I warned in the Introduction, some of the bigger 'issues' in this guide are a bit weightier than others. And learning the ropes when buying property is about as weighty and important as it gets – because *what* you buy, *why* you buy it, *where* you buy and *how much* you pay is absolutely pivotal to getting this business right.

Forget everything you've previously read or been told. This guide takes you back to the very beginning of the learning curve that's part and parcel of knowing 'enough' not to fail. **Investing wisely is a 'mindset' thing.**

You need to pick over the bones of your thinking with a care and honesty you probably haven't realised. Therefore, reading this lesson takes time. But it's time well spent. In fact it's absolutely essential time. Believe me, if the amount of time merely reading about the reality daunts you, remember that the lettings business is a long-term investment, it's a big step involving big money over even bigger timescales.

So what you first have to realise is that **anyone can be a landlord. It's being a successful landlord that counts.**

However, to unpick an industry this diverse means that some earlier lessons are inevitably weightier than others.

Knowing what to buy

Why does what I buy matter?

Because bad property choices just aren't easy to fix.

Does it really matter that much?

Nothing is irredeemable, but 'hard' properties with inadequate 'markets' are the most difficult problems to 'solve'.

It's now virtually impossible to offer the 'wrong' type of lease or for tenants to outstay their welcome, but it remains horribly simple to buy the wrong building because you didn't understand the market.

The climate that you invest in matters. A lot!

Despite all you've ever read before, snapping up any old unit with no idea of the local market conditions is a recipe for problems, long void periods, disruptive tenants, poor rent flow. Bananas won't grow in Surrey, grapes might, apples will. Understanding local climates matters. **Everything in this first lesson is either important, necessary, or absolutely vital**.

Letting property is no get rich quick scheme – it's a long-haul slog. Research and understanding of what's right for you are paramount. It's not your job to fill your agent's window with yet another un-let property that he advised you to buy when wearing his estate agent's hat. It is your job to find the right match to your own unique circumstances for such a long-term purchase.

Why is buying the 'right' property so important?

Because paying vast sums of money for the wrong building is the most costly mistake you can make.

What's the first step?

For most landlords (but by no means all), the first part of the process usually boils down to buying one or more properties, and that means making choices in what is a fantastically diverse market.

What kind of tenancies should I be considering?

Assured shortholds – no question about it. (For details of what they are, how they work and what few exceptions can't be shortholds, read Lesson 5: Assured shorthold leases.)

Why does it matter what kind of tenancy I use?

Because, when using shorthold assured tenancies (ie those created by the 1988 Housing Acts), landlords are guaranteed under the law that their property will be returned at the end of a relatively short initial 'fixed term', therefore (a bit of hassle aside) that part of things simply cannot go too far wrong.

Can anything go wrong?

Indeed but all businesses have running 'issues' occasionally. That's par for the course. What's important is the structure of the business investment whether your business is tenants or timeshares.

Nothing that you do, or even that backfires a bit is anything like as troublesome as buying an inappropriate property nor as hard to correct.

Unfortunately, that knack of making a wise investment choice simply isn't down to 'luck' or finding one of those mythical 'snips'. Research takes time. With it, you can find the right match in tenant types or pocket size to suit any safe building.

A vital word on safety

Without exceptions or excuses, absolutely everything that a landlord lets to a tenant *must* be safe. And that means safe as defined by a variety of legislation (housing, health and safety, common and civil and now HMO (houses in multiple occupation) and deposit rules to name but a few – see appropriate lessons). Safe does *not* mean what your brother-in-law's builder claims is 'safe'. Safety needs to be built into every rental unit. Forget it at your peril.

Problem buildings

But be warned, rental research requires an absolute honesty that's quite opposite to the qualities that so many of us use to survive other work environments. Something is wrong with rent levels, location, presentation or management style when buildings are repeatedly empty or attract problematic tenants. Learn to look on problems as questions needing solutions and *find* some.

What types of property should I consider?

Buying investment property requires you to consider a huge range of topics simultaneously. The tired old advice of 'snapping up a two-bedroomed flat on the next development' that so many novices have listened to, has led to a crisis of gluts and falling rents that should never have occurred had investors been encouraged to examine the whole, huge marketplace – to say nothing of overpriced new developments that can push both you and your lender straight into negative equity before you've even taken hold of the keys!

Before you buy brand new, check out selling prices for similar flats locally that are six to 12 months old. Forget the cars, two-year deals and free carpets. They're peanuts on a cost base of £200,000. Many nearly new units are trading at around 30 per cent cheaper than new asking prices – but their rent level will usually be exactly the same.

Whatever the property, the questions remain the same

- Is the price of the unit viable?
- Is it suitable for borrowings?
- Is it affordable in your circumstances?
- Is it in a safe condition without massive expense?
- Is it likely to create an HMO (read Lesson 13 on HMOs dedicated to these potentially radical changes)?
- Are you looking for instant profit over costs, ie high yield?
- Or are you looking for long-term capital acquisition (overall return)?
- Are you prepared to cross-subsidise borrowing costs from other income? Or not?

But the most vital question to landlords is: will this unit attract a decade's worth of *customers*? *Because tenants, not buildings, pay rent.*

What skills will I need to be a successful landlord?

Solid people skills

Letting property is – almost above all else – a 'people business'. Even if you never intend meeting a single tenant, buying a temporary home for someone else requires you to have some idea of how they live. Only then can you match what type of management you'll need, to what you (or your agent) can provide.

And be realistic

There simply aren't enough 'professional non-smoking high-earning cleanliness freaks' out there to sustain your hopes let alone an entire industry.

Successful investors make informed decisions. They don't guess, or take advice from a kid in a letting's agency. They know – long before they buy – a skill that you need to start acquiring long before you start spending.

Rush buys can be mistakes. Guesswork is for the foolish. And auction bargains are for experts – not beginners.

What this statement means is that you need to know long before you purchase a thing who your prospective tenants might be, for what kind of money and whether this figure will match the figures you have in mind to make your goals work. For a decade at least.

Never embark on the understanding (or let an agent convince you) that there'll be wild rent hikes just down the line – that ball has rolled. You need to become self-reliant in order not to become someone else's commission groupie. So here's a timely anecdote!

WARNING ANECDOTE

I expressed interest in a petite three-bedroomed Georgian building in the poshest part of a small town. Given the family's name has long been associated with lettings, the agent promptly contacted their in-house letting's service. By the time of my viewing, the estate agent handed me a card from their valuations manager with his company's estimate of the likely rent we could charge.

This enthusiastic lettings department were glibly quoting rent levels of – at the very least – one third above the maximum I could ever have achieved. And, what's particularly galling is that, had I been new to the business, or an out-of-town investor and believed this ludicrous over-valuation was realistic, I could have lost a small fortune until I dropped the rent level to anything like a reasonable rate for the area.

Unfortunately, because there's no genuine profession involved, those churning out such reckless advice cannot be struck off. The letting industry is a 'you eat what you kill' culture. Be careful you're not someone else's three-course lunch.

(Foolproof instructions on how to do rental valuations long before you buy are in Lesson 2: Mock advertising.)

How much will I be able to borrow?

Thinking the above anecdote through logically, takes us to another industry issue.

Many lenders rely on letting agency rent valuations and use factors of 130 per cent to calculate how much they're willing to lend. Now, it's all well and good oiling the wheels of your deal – but this type of borrowing can't be based on pie in the sky figures. Rentals are supposed to make money for landlords somewhere along the way. What Buy to Let (BTL) should never be allowed to become is a way to obtain sales for estate agents. Or a commission generator for mortgage advisors. Nor indeed another way for lenders to encourage overheated borrowings. **Never forget you're not the only one here who's looking to make a profit.**

Banks don't 'lend' . . . they 'rent' money. Of course, that wouldn't look quite so attractive on the posters and leaflets – so the nice linguistic 'lending' has been hijacked. Take nothing at face value, especially not a willingness to 'lend' against a property. What's the lender got to lose? You provide them a nice little cushion by putting up the first 20 per cent. Plus, they get interest monthly. If the whole thing goes belly up, tell me who has the most to lose – you or the lender?

First find your customers

Pricing buildings for sale or calculating likely rent is not a precise science. How much rent you'll actually receive on any type of unit depends on the local supply of tenants – and on nothing else. (See Lesson 2: Mock advertising to learn how to value before you spend one penny.)

WARNING ANECDOTE

Recently I ran a class for new investors. Each week, Maria turned up. Having withdrawn a lifetime's equity from her home, she'd invested in two new flats. Each week, she worried that her flats had no tenants. Each week, I asked her to consider dropping the rent. Each week she insisted that agents had told her that she could command the rents she was asking and explained – at length – how attractive they were. Each week, she lost more money. My course lasted 13 weeks. Maria had no tenants for any of that time. Her self-belief was commendable. Her economics lamentable. Week by week, Maria was slowly bankrupting herself because she genuinely believed that rental units had fixed values. They don't. Something is only worth what someone else will pay for it.

What market opportunities genuinely exist?

The market opportunities are vast – enormous – behemoth – colossal. Remember the old adage 'it takes all types', well never more so than when servicing tenants.

There is a vast range of tenants looking for homes. Some tenants are as rich as Croesus, some are very poor, and most fall somewhere in between. The ultimate determinant for landlords and tenants alike is money. Therefore learning to crunch your numbers with reasonable accuracy is essential.

This is a customer business. And that's the only consideration that matters – because the only way to make money in the let property game is to have a good supply of them. That way the worst that can happen is that tenants will – over time purchase a building for you! Not a bad premise. (And if this isn't your first premise you should be looking at the other, equally valid, investment types of property speculation/development, which are quicker but riskier.)

How do I begin my research?

Think about what tenants there are in the areas that interest you

Decide realistically what slice of this vast market you'd be servicing within your budget. Clearly, the higher the budget the greater the range of options. But all the types identified here offer real investment opportunities.

Low cost units or shared housing

Less affluent tenants always have and always will fill rental property in less affluent areas. Low waged (or even no waged) tenants walk further to catch the bus or tube to save money. And believe me, low waged tenants are much thicker on the ground than well off ones. What's more, landlords servicing this end of the market positively flourish. Youngsters don't always dust much – or bleach the loo – but they pay out billions in rent each year. However, shared units are about to feel the hot breath of the new HMO laws, so you might prefer to buy into smaller units. The ideal rental unit is usually a studio or one-bedroom flat, though these aren't necessarily the best bet for capital appreciation. *Quid pro quo*.

Most shared accommodation works on a collaborative basis and is often wrongly regarded as exclusively a young people business. But many older adults thrive in bed sits (where each unit offers a degree of privacy and separation but some facilities are shared). It may surprise you, but there's a real place for this niche housing all over the country – even when costs of complying with HMO regulations are factored into the equation.

WARNING ANECDOTE

Don't judge a book by its cover. The unlikeliest people can make brilliant tenants. One of my best tenant recommendations was written about a newly married couple in a modest bed-sitter arrangement. Both had learning difficulties. Both worked as night cleaners. But their preparation for life outside institutional care had made them excellent managers of their own environment and their limited money.

Families

Families are as rare as hen's teeth in the private rental sector. Some landlords do incredibly well by working in partnership with housing associations or local authorities; usually offering accommodation to what's inaccurately referred to as DSS but what's actually the Housing Benefit end of the market. Many housing associations, local authorities and charities offer Head Lease Schemes to landlords, where (given the building meets certain standards) they, (sooner than any individual family), become your tenants and take over all management and repair functions, leaving you with nothing more to do than bank their regular cheques. These arrangements can offer excellent long-term renewable contracts of around five years, where rent is guaranteed by the organisation and they also guarantee to return your property at the end of the contract in good condition.

There is a limited middle-income family market – though in general most people prefer owning to renting when they need security for their children. Landlords embarking on buying property for the family market need to realise that the market is limited and a three-bedroom semi without a family may often become a house share or sit empty.

Landlords considering buying for sharers and all existing landlords need to factor in the costs of full statutory compliance and new annual Licences into their purchase/maintenance/refurbishment figures (see Lesson 13: Houses in Multiple Occupation). Sharers will still *always* occupy a large proportion of the market because demand is huge – so long as you are completely realistic about safety requirements.

The student market

Student landlords are another independent breed, who, up and down the country, do very nicely from their slice of student borrowings. Others wouldn't touch it with poles.

But be wary. Many universities have made long-term commitments to creaming this money off for their own coffers and have huge building projects underway. If so, think about how you'll compete before you buy. With a steady pool of freshers and worried parents who watched *Rising Damp*, universities are in a much stronger competitive position than the average student landlord is.

Good student landlords are a hardy breed. They'll don rubber gloves and wield paintbrushes at the end of term to keep themselves competitive in a frisky market. But successful student landlords need more than that. They need to understand and probably like young people who don't always behave as well as they might and who are often under enormous financial pressures. They also require the financial restraint to build a healthy bank balance between September and June.

Whatever niche you choose, property is *never* a quickie.

Do be wary of the university admissions department suggesting that you 'buy to let' for the duration of your daughter's degree. These set up and disposal costs only make sense over a period of years. Prices may well have peaked in areas where this idea was ever viable. Beyond those issues – friends fall out. Your daughter will make a lousy landlord and won't have the skills to manage her new friends. And the taxman will certainly come after any genuine rise in property value at punitive rates. Do the sums – factor in your absence after three short years and walk away if you can't make the numbers crunch for ten!

Mid-priced units

Many landlords live and operate in the mid range of the market. Here, you'll find hundreds of thousands of tenants on a renewing basis each year – who do thankfully – fall into a few main groups.

Under 35s

Often single or in couples/pairs, these tenants are looking for smallish units that are decent, convenient and affordable. But ignore all the two beds as a must 'puff'. Most tenants can't afford to rent a spare room. Tenants tend to rent the minimum that they need, not what they aspire to.

Over 50s

Often male and often with wives wanting a short bit of breathing space. Snatch them up fast – they can make excellent long-term tenants. Or you may be letting to new, older couples. Nest leavers will pay a small premium for something with a few of the comforts they're used to at home but not too many – cost can be a real eye opener to a guy whose wife did all the decorating. I still have a tenant who fits both the above categories and he's been a tenant since 1989. Good tenant selection, you can't beat it!

The huge miscellaneous category

Then there are all the other people who don't fall into any particular category. People who move job and who need to bed into an area. People who work from a small unit then go home for weekends. People trying out new lives. Families with 2.4 kids and a Labrador testing out local areas. One or two adulterers (believe it or not in this day and age) who want a little place 'on the quiet'! As landlords, you'll meet them all. And I guarantee that you'll be pleasantly surprised at just how many really nice people there are out there who want nothing more than a decent place to live with a fair minded landlord. Most have no intention of trashing the place. And, despite what you hear, the vast majority of tenants live, pay rent, give notice, clean up and then move on.

High cost units

There is one caveat to the logic of becoming an independent landlord that covers this small niche. Wealthy tenants demand their money's worth. High value units invariably have very demanding tenants who equally require very intensive management. If this is the niche you're hoping to service, you'll need more than hope to survive. The tiny ultra rich share of the market remains the almost exclusive territory of one or two highly specialised and long-standing agencies that have a century or more of experience in handling the (mainly London) mega rich bracket. And gosh, can this type of tenant play hardball. Many landlords come to grief by investing heavily – but still falling well short of what these tenants demand. It's a tough cookie to crack and not cost effective for most landlords.

WARNING ANECDOTE

I did a brief consultative stint at a 'top shop' behind Harrods and discovered that not a single unit had Gas Safety Certificates (even expired ones). The confident Hong Kong investor who owned the place thought that the safety regulations were for poor tenants. Every rental unit in England and Wales carries exactly the same liabilities for safety and sharing that their cheaper colleagues enjoy. Housing legislation is an equal opportunities kind of fella. I wonder what they'll make of the new HMO regulations?

So, what are landlords hoping to find?

One or more properties in appropriate locations that satisfy that timeless business equation.

Time + market conditions + regulations = a chance to succeed

How to check out what you're being told by agents and others

Do not allow the local estate or lettings agent to quote crazy prices and wildly optimistic yields without checking them yourself. Believe nothing that can't be proved – and preferably get everything in writing. Ask to see signed leases which prove these high rent level estimates. Check what prices recent properties have sold for by checking on the Land Registry website for factual information.

Choosing the right property at the right price can take ages. Worthwhile research takes time, accurate information and very steady nerves. That old cliché 'spend for pleasure, repent at leisure' just about sums up this business.

So, how do I make good choices?

Having decided what property niches in the area interest you, it's time to start detailed checking. Read the local property to let columns thoroughly and find properties that sound similar to the ones that interest you. Isolate areas of interest and start walking. What kind of area is it? What kind of property round there is the norm? Beware of tying to buck local trends. Doing up a house beautifully will not improve its location or even necessarily the rent. Improvements need to be included in your overall setting up costs – so think carefully before you buy (nor are they tax deductible until you sell, see Lesson 15: The tax man's take). Be ruthlessly realistic about how much rent you'll achieve locally by mock advertising. Rental norms for the area will always outweigh your efforts with a paintbrush.

Checking out a chosen area

When looking to buy cheaper housing

If you're searching relatively cheap areas watch out for red light districts. Decent single women will know where they are and avoid them like the plague, making them difficult to let (except to working girls) and believe it or not – most young men don't like being endlessly propositioned all the way home every night.

In every town centre or city location, visit during the day on weekdays and weekends – and go back at night. Some areas can change dramatically after nightfall. Difficult areas tend to be tricky to let (euphemism for cheap!). You may still want to buy there but avoid paying 'top dollar'. Beware agents telling you an area's 'on the up' – they always say that.

Trust your instincts. If you have enough acumen to be buying a second building, you're not a stupid person. Believe what you see, not what you've been told. Trust me, your potential tenants will be looking very carefully before they rent.

Never lose sight of the fact that you'll need a steady stream of customers for at least a decade. Whether this property will regularly attract customers is the only criteria that counts.

Ex-council property

Large council blocks may produce low priced units, which may be (but often aren't) easy to let. But what if they attract nothing like the local area's average capital appreciation? Make especially sure that local tenants will be willing to rent in the environment by mock advertising.

Ex-local authority flats can be cheaper than those on the open market but that local authority is your freeholder. Bear in mind the council's departments can be slow to respond to problems – legal or maintenance. Your leaking windows might make this investment completely un-lettable but that won't necessarily cut much ice with a huge organisation whose purpose is to house the needy – not running around after investors with burned fingers. This kind of investment has been popularised lately by a few journalists but this type of letting is significantly more hassle in every respect, despite a bit of good press. Expect delays at every stage – including resale. Go for it by all means if it suits you – but not because you were under-informed.

Check the facilities and the amenities

In large cities, check transport links – your tenants certainly will. If you need to use a lift in a block of flats – does it work? Did it work last week? If you're looking in a private sector block at a leasehold, try knocking on a door or two and asking questions. Ask what the freeholder is like. Are they reasonable or do they have a track record of unnecessary works and billing their long-suffering leaseholders? Does that expensive lease actually prevent you subletting? Are there any other rentals in the block? Ask how often they are empty.

In smaller blocks, some leaseholders intensely dislike private rentals and they can make your tenant's life quite uncomfortable. Best find out first, or spend unnecessary time endlessly re-letting. Be nice – then be nosey.

That three-bedroom house on the pleasant private estate might be a low price because the area's nice enough but the local school's appalling. If your target market is families this could be a problem. Find out *before* you buy. If your target market is, say, 25-year-old sharers – it may not matter. But will they want to spend every weekend surrounded by other people's screaming kids? Or might this lower the demand/rent?

How to squeeze detail from the information you've been given

A good estate agent won't tell you he's trying to shift a stale or overpriced property. So you'll also need a keen eye for detail. Take a good look at the leaflets. What season do they show? Knock on the door and ask the vendor how long the property's been up for sale – without the agent's canny advice, they'll often tell the truth. If not – ask the neighbours. Again, I emphasise, people skills are a must in every aspect of this type of investment. Being nosey can save you a fortune.

A warning for the unwary

Never believe the guff about a new employer moving into town, or a new road connecting nowhere to somewhere – unless you can see them actually digging the foundations. Estate agents are like spiders, they can't help spinning.

Are there good and bad times to buy investment property?

Not especially – it's a number crunch thing. It remains an excellent way to acquire money that you don't now have. Some people have cash – say from a deal or an inheritance. Others are looking to borrow. Everyone's circumstances vary so there's no fixed right or wrong. The only thing that should affect your decision is tenant supply at rent levels that make your own numbers work.

Once you think you've found something appropriate

Take a step back mentally and think it through.

How good is the area? What type of person lives round there? Be honest – is what you can afford in a ropey area? If so, that's likely to determine the type of tenants you'll attract – so – does that bother you? If the investment's sound – it shouldn't.

Property investors need to be completely dispassionate. You won't be living here yourself and you might hope your daughter doesn't – but that's not the issue. Investment in property is about sums – will yours work here – or won't they?

Buying a more attractive property might seem more appealing. However, that smart house might not generate as much monthly return as two cheaper units. Indeed, there's a great deal to commend several cheaper units as it spreads risk and improves cash flow.

WARNING ANECDOTE

There's been a great deal of press coverage lately about numerous 'new' schemes – aimed at people with little or no rental experience. But giving money to strangers – or investing in schemes run by strangers over which you have no direct control can be very risky. Schemes like these get media attention because they're novel – not necessarily because they are good ideas. Check and check again. 'Look before you leap' isn't a cliché for nothing.

Finally, time to crunch numbers one last time

If you're still happy with your proposal in principle, it's now crunch time, and time to do a full-scale financial analysis. Paper and pen time. Make two columns – Credits and Debits. Pour yourself a strong gin and tonic.

Note, use this handy weekly equation to convert all costs into weekly costs:

Divide annual costs by 52 = weekly cost

Multiply monthly costs by twelve then divide by 52 = weekly cost

For example:

Annual costs are £850 per annum insurance cost
= £850 divided by 52 = £16.35 per week

Per calendar month costs are £1,000 per calendar month rent
= £1,000 × 12 divided by 52 = £230.77 per week

(P.c.m. rents are a recent 'innovation' used by agents because that helps their accounting systems – historically and in established agencies, rents are charged weekly for reasons explained later but which generate slightly more income.)

Credits column

This is how much rent you're realistically likely to receive per week. Now put that weekly rent into your credit column. And that's it. Next comes the really scary bit.

Debits column

Until you get used to doing this, I've broken some of your costs down to remind you what you may need to include. Cheating to make your numbers balance is a fool's game – be accurate. Initially, costs need to be subdivided. All should be included in a long-term plan but realistically; most novices swallow initial set up costs (but set up costs have to be funded sometime – unless you believe in fairies).

Purchase costs

These are usually one-off costs per unit. To include them divide each amount by the length of the loan term (say 20 years), before dividing by 52 to get a weekly cost over the term of the investment.

Include where applicable:

- Stamp duty.
- Legal fees.
- Finder's fees (if applicable).
- Mortgage fees.
- Valuation fees.
- Insurance on loan costs (if applicable).
- Plus, most lenders will expect borrowers to pay a minimum of 20 per cent deposit – so lost interest on that capital is an ongoing expense until you sell and recoup that loss.
- Other costs incurred.

Set-up costs

These are costs which may/may not occur on an annual or any other regular basis.

Include what's applicable only to your unit and convert into weekly costs:

- Initial refurbishment and any works required to make the building suitable and safe for letting. Note, keep to maintenance and upgrades wherever possible. Improvements (like installing central heating where none existed previously) are not tax deductible until you sell.

- Surveyor's fees (optional yes – but a godsend for schedules of conditions and for driving down the purchase price if pressing matters are highlighted).

- Furniture, carpets, cookers, other white goods.

- Other safety equipment – smoke alarms, extinguishers, fire blankets certified electrical check, gas safety where applicable.

Annual running costs

Almost all are tax deductible in the tax year.

Use the earlier equation to convert annual and monthly costs.

- **Monthly borrowing costs**
  Borrowings have two components: interest and capital repayments. Both must be included here for a realistic equation. Some investors are being encouraged to work out their figures on 'interest only' mortgage costs. And so I repeat – you are not playing games here – your full costs need to be included. Borrowings need to be repaid – and hoping that soaring property prices will bail you out is playing with fire and isn't an appropriate strategy for investors.

- **Loss of interest**
  Boring I know, but if you've cashed in that 20 per cent deposit from an interest bearing investment or account, the loss of that interest is a real cost. If you've borrowed against your home, include the full monthly costs of the equity drawdown in weekly chunks.

- **Ground rent and service charges (for leasehold properties).**

- **Insurance costs**
  Landlords are advised to consult carefully that insurance will be available *long before* they purchase. Many areas of lettings (especially multi-occupied buildings and housing benefit claimants) are tricky to insure. Other areas where radon gas or flooding are issues are becoming very difficult to insure and no landlord can operate safely without insurance. Insure only the building, landlord liabilities and your contents. Tenants must insure their own goods. (Younger tenants sometimes find this difficult – suggest that they add their contents to their parent's insurance policy.) Landlords need specialist insurance – a simple buildings and contents policy is not enough. Most brokers will advise you.

- **Building maintenance costs**
  Depending on the age and condition of property – between five and ten per cent of income per year ongoing for major repairs.

- **Service contracts.**

- **Void periods**
  Usually advised at 6–8 weeks per annum (but work like the devil to avoid them).

- **Annual accounts**
  Unless you know enough to do your own, which most of us don't, consult a professional (see Lesson 15: The tax man's take).

- **Sundries**
  Telephone calls, legal stationery, travel, postage, council tax at 50 per cent for empty periods (about to be phased out so expect 100 per cent costs soon).

- **Advertising**
  Always keep receipts or credit card statements.

- **All management costs or tenant find costs (if applicable).**

- **Annual gas safety certification.**

- **Annual inventory costs**
  The only person who works for free is you – so the more you learn, the more profit you keep. (See Lesson 7: Inventory, Schedules of Condition and Property Profiles.)

■ **Four full sets of keys.**

■ **Lease costs**
   These should be minimal (see Lesson 5: Assured shorthold leases) unless tailor-made.

■ **Licensing fees for all multiply occupied buildings**
   (See Lesson 13: Houses in Multiple Occupation.)

■ **Unless you fancy working for love**
   Try throwing a minimum wage at your hours – just for fun.

■ **A sense of humour and proportion**
   Last – but by no means least – these cost nothing and have the potential to save you a small fortune. Breakdown in landlord/tenant/agent relationships are one of the most costly issues that you can avoid – no charge – but which can set costs soaring if underdeveloped. Don't take things personally. Your tenant really didn't flood out the bathroom to spite you. And if you own furniture which you've lovingly polished for a decade don't put it in a rental.

Note, most private landlords are entitled to other deductions for wear and tear at ten per cent per annum (see Lesson 15: The tax man's take).

By now, you should have two columns, one of which is depressingly short – the other of which is startlingly long. Hold your nerve – they always look like this.

Do I know enough to invest wisely yet?

Only invest if your bottom lines tally – that is the income equals the expenditure. If they don't, pull out unless you have other finances in place to subsidise the deal.

Why using genuine professionals matters when purchasing investments

Unless you are very experienced, shift liability – wherever possible – onto the insurance policies of genuine professionals. Time and time again, I see and hear or read advice to scrimp on things like surveys.

What this ridiculous advice overlooks is what you're actually buying. Buy a survey report (at £500 it's a fraction of one per cent of most property transactions). And with it comes the assurance that if anything major is wrong with the building and they report on it, you can renegotiate the price. If it's been missed, you have comeback because that report carries indemnity. Similarly, the same applies to solicitors. For landlords, especially those of you buying leasehold units, don't scrimp on a cheap solicitor. This is false economy. You need a good solicitor and give them a written list of the questions that you have about your rights and responsibilities before you commit yourself.

Break open a file – you'll need it

Now is also the time to break open a file (one per property). Owning, running and maintaining property generates a paper-trail and you need to keep accurate records.

Landlords considering buying leasehold properties

Ask your solicitor to check out the management operation of leasehold property and to explain your liabilities under the lease in detail and in writing to avoid 'confusion' later.

Check leasehold terms carefully

Read leases carefully and understand what you're getting into *before* you sign. Many leases have strange caveats – some refuse to have rental tenants at all – some won't allow stripped floors because of overhead noise (especially those constructed before the major Building Regulation changes in 1992). The list is endless. Know exactly what you're buying.

If you're considering a 'share of freehold' contact the other sharers before you proceed to see what they're like. Do they get on? Are they cliquey? If so, can you be bothered with the endless angst? They can make a tenant's life hell if so inclined.

Freehold properties

Assume nothing. Freeholds can also have weird caveats, clauses, easements and the like buried in the endless Title Deeds. Registered land (bought or sold since the 1970s) has a summary of idiosyncrasies.

Get your solicitor to check carefully for potential problems.

WARNING ANECDOTE

An unwary investor decided to purchase property and was using it to offer some bed and breakfast and occasional short lodgings. Her neighbours took exception to what was a negligible increase in traffic into her drive. Collectively they paid a solicitor to invoke an ancient clause forbidding the running of any form of business on all the surrounding land. This clause – inserted into the Title Deeds by the former owners, way back in the 1800s – had never been deleted. The whole matter escalated into a tribunal hearing. The investor lost to her neighbours who were awarded thousands of pounds worth of damages, enough to virtually bankrupt the investor, who was obliged to sell up and cash in precious equity to pay them all off.

How to use that full structural survey to best advantage

Make all offers 'subject to survey'. That steady surveyor is probably the only voice of reason you'll hear amongst the babble of commission-hungry voices, disinterested lenders and over-excited vendors. What your buddy the builder says won't cut much mustard. But, brandishing a full, professionally insured and signed report from a qualified professional is excellent peace of mind, gives you someone to sue if problems have been missed and remains the best tool there is for hammering down the purchase price.

Having paid for a survey *read it*. A good survey will point out problems with drains, wiring or plumbing as well as the roof and foundations. Running a building is exactly like running a car – some items wear out and need replacement – but all cost more than a new tyre. Be aware of the long-term issues in your building – and plan in costs.

Handling the purchase process

Get a written list of everything included in the sale from the vendor and make sure the estate agent explains what 'fixtures and fittings' means to his client. Everything that's fixed to the wall and that is being removed (mirrors, shelves, wardrobes, etc.) must be declared in writing by the seller.

WARNING ANECDOTE

The first purchase I made was an eye opener. Before moving out the vendor removed every nice doorknob, leaving doors with holes. He then thoughtfully cut off every single electrical fitting hanging in the room from the roses. I wished him death by electrocution for the entire costly week where the electrician rewired the whole lighting circuit (including ripping up every upstairs floorboard for access). People can *always* surprise you! Get it in writing.

If vendors then steal what you have agreed to purchase in the deal, get your solicitor to demand restitution. If all else fails, sue them in the small claims court. Conversely, buildings should be emptied of everything that belongs to the seller that you haven't asked him to leave. If they leave behind them several unpleasant divans and a shed full of tat follow the same procedure.

A bitter reality on the ground

Before we move on, there is an issue that I feel obliged to mention particularly for novice landlords, who know little of the lettings sector. Historically, the low end of lettings has been a hidden industry, one that has functioned for decades unseen and unregulated (maybe the new laws will change this?). The characteristics of independence and being able to 'row one's own boat' have, unfortunately attracted some very unsavoury characters into the business. Individuals who feel that rules apply to everyone but them, and unfortunately, they're often right! Whilst the local authority will chase a decent landlord's tail over what can seem like minor indiscretions – these scoundrel landlords are rarely tackled by the man from the council.

Here's a timely anecdote – I've no idea how representative it is – however, it did happen in a town where I cut my letting's teeth – and I doubt it's unique.

WARNING ANECDOTE

Large properties in shoddy parts of towns have always been used for lettings by the room with shared toilets, etc. Bedsit land. Where decent landlords sit shoulder to shoulder with some unscrupulous colleagues. An area was targeted by one large, extended family. They bought several properties let out to single men on Housing Benefit. Gradually, over months, other landlords in nearby houses and roads were 'asked' to sell up. Those who declined were shamelessly intimidated – gangs of threatening yobs followed tenants home suggesting that they 'move on' because 'there's going to be trouble'.

Word spread and soon decent landlords found it difficult to find new tenants. Angry, they telephoned an uninterested police station. Eventually, the few landlords who remained, were terrorised when visiting their own properties. Tyres were slashed. There was jostling as they walked down streets. Within three short years, every landlord in four lengthy streets filled with huge four-storey buildings had accepted a ludicrously low offer from one or other member of 'the family', to salvage what they could.

So be wary. If you're considering this type of investment, check online at the Land Registry www.landregistryonline.gov.uk. Do a £2 search on the addresses nearby – and look for a good spread of names. Don't buy in an area that may be operating as a cartel. You'll regret it.

Housing Benefit and Head Lease Schemes

Even with the best efforts of some local councils, the core of many of the North's towns are dying. People with wages are no longer willing to settle for a bleak terraced house and a bleaker back yard. So be realistic. This type of housing is almost invariably Housing Benefit territory. Which raises another issue. Social housing is almost always best provided/managed by local authorities with social work skills. Their tenants are often vulnerable people with complex social issues, heavy drinking, old age, substance abuse, mental illness and a myriad of financial pressures which accompany them.

We've all read stories of articles alleging 'huge capital growth potential'. Some of them may even be true. But good rental units need a solid local economy of jobs and wages to underpin them. Without that, where are your customers?

Buying cheap property in former industrial towns can work well, especially if you can let it out through housing associations and local authorities via Head Lease Schemes. They offer guaranteed, long-term contracts, which include all management. The Housing Benefit sector remains undoubtedly lucrative – however, do check two things *well in advance* of plunging headlong into this type of purchase:

1. That the local authorities/housing associations actually need further supply. Many don't.

2. That your lender will agree to this form of tenancy.

Beware of 'too good to be true' prices in distant places

It can look very tempting on paper – buy up a couple of tatty terraces, spruce them up and reap the rewards. But be realistic. Two hundred miles away can be an awfully long round trip to do viewings so you have to use costly agents. The best advice for the novice is probably to cut one's teeth more locally. Building your national portfolio can always come later.

Here's a timely tale – told to me by an agent with a very broad grin.

WARNING ANECDOTE

Old terraced housing can be very chilly and finding tenants willing to shiver in front of a single bar of an electric fire can be difficult, especially in areas where outside investors have flooded the market with this type of cheap housing, looking for a killing. Undeterred, this agent had been marketing heavily in the local press and had, in the space of months, taken over 70 new properties onto his books. This agent had cornered a captive market – most of whom lived hundreds of miles away.

Of course, oversupply drives down rents (we're talking £60–£75 per week for a three-bedroom house in some areas), so many properties languished, empty for months.

His solution? To insist that every landlord installed central heating or be removed from his books. By using his own in-house Corgi registered contractors at rates way above the usual local cost, he made a tidy profit of more than £1,000 on every single unit. Many are still empty. He still charges all these hog-tied landlords for routine inspections, regular redecorations, safety certificates and whatever else he can think of.

Never underestimate the inventive nature of an entrepreneur. Forget fat cat landlords, agents have found more ways to skin cats than you'd believe.

A few final tips

- Only the self-reliant survive in this market.

- Look everywhere and into everything before you choose your own niche. There are plenty of opportunities for investment, and plenty of pitfalls to avoid. Remember – you're looking for customers, *not* premises per se.

- Believe what you see and read – not what you're told by a salesman.

- Bad or incomplete advice is plentiful – good advice is scarcer.

- There is no 'one size fits all' in the lettings' business. It's a bespoke kind of business.

Time to choose

Happy with your well-researched choice, feeling plucky and still fancying chancing your arm for some of HM Revenue & Customs legendary 'unearned income'? Then it's time to start tackling the nuts and bolts of becoming a fully-fledged private landlord. As promised – after the undoubted hassle of finding the right property, I guarantee that everything else will seem like a piece of cake!

And finally − some advice to those of you who wish to avoid the costs of using agencies.

Distance management

There's always a way to avoid agency costs. But it does take careful planning. I've set up perfectly viable lets for landlords who simply couldn't afford to use agents. The secret here is realistic planning and foresight. Distance management is a viable alternative that works perfectly well for those who fancy independence but can't afford local agents.

Tips to make it work effectively

- Interview extensively, scrutinise several tenants thoroughly before choosing.

- Take careful references − Tenant Application Forms, bank/employer/character and especially credit checks. (See Lesson 9: Selecting tenants and tying up the deal). Double check with phone calls.

- You'll need a small team of local friends or relatives, each to be responsible for small areas. Don't overwhelm any one person. One person needs to be contactable for essential repairs (to authorise repairs − or not). Bank statements need to be set up for three days after each rent payment should have arrived. You'll also need someone local to agree to act as key-holder. Friendly neighbours work best or a security firm will oblige.

- Insure everything possible and set up service contracts for all that you can (boilers can be sorted out with British Gas to include an annual Landlord's Gas Safety Certificate).

- Notify mortgage lender and insurers.

- Serve a Prior Notice 1 − (see Lesson 11: Ending tenancies, for details).

- Store private/precious items somewhere else.

- Approach a local plumber, locksmith and electrician. Find people willing to work and send bills to a friend left holding a small financial float of say £500.

■ Compile thorough inventories and Schedules of Condition and always provide a comprehensive Property Profile (see Lesson 7: Inventories, Schedules of Condition and Property Profiles).

Tenancies like these can and do work well. Most tenants are decent people who want somewhere decent to live. Look carefully and the chances are that you'll find some.

Whys and wherefores

There's a huge amount of support for the advice in this lengthy lesson. Ignore agency websites and blurb. There are genuine experts all around you to learn from (especially other independents who've been doing the business for donkey's years) that cost little or nothing. Look online: www.landlordline.co.uk, www.RICS.co.uk, www.RLA.org.uk or www.lawrights.co.uk are particularly useful, user friendly websites: you'll find many more. Alternatively, join your local Small Landlords Association for impartial advice. There's a rich seam of reasonable advice in some of the reputable newspapers. Try national newspapers online and head for their archive section – then type in a few key words. Research is as big a beast as you want it to be – but there's no shortage of good advice out there – if you bother to look. A final suggestion is the investment in a single book on landlord and tenant law – and the *Which Guide to Renting and Letting* is a must.

— CHECKLIST/SUMMARY —

■ Anyone can be a landlord – it's being a successful landlord that counts.

■ Rental properties need customers.

■ Buildings don't pay rent – that's what tenants are for.

■ Make sure that your property is *safe*. Specific legislation exists to protect your tenants and, in many areas, much more is coming on-stream. Besides which, they're your customers – they *deserve* to be safe.

■ This is a people business, learn some people skills.

■ Anyone can manage any property independently – agents are a luxury, or convenience – never a necessity.

- Tenant demand is pivotal to every decision you make. Ignore it at your peril. The lettings' business takes no prisoners.

- Rent levels follow the Retail Price Index – not house price inflation and tenants know local norms. How much you paid for a property won't affect its rental value.

- Tenant types are as diverse as building types. Don't limit yourself to two-bedroom flats 'because everyone wants that'. It's not true.

- Tenant demand covers every single aspect of the price range – be certain what type of tenant is a good match and that demand still exists for your particular investment before you buy.

- Property is never 'a quickie'. Be prepared for a ten-year minimum commitment.

- Check areas thoroughly – before you buy.

- Be nosey. Knock on doors and ask questions. People are by nature, chatty, friendly and nice.

- When crunching your numbers, be ruthlessly honest. Deluding yourself is a fool's game.

- Build a void period of 6–8 weeks into costings – then fight to keep your unit filled all 52 weeks.

- Empty units are your problem waiting to be solved! Find a solution. This is a punishing market for slow movers.

- Get building advice and written reports from a *qualified professional.*

- Get tax advice from a qualified professional – they know ways to minimise liabilities.

- No cheating now. *Read the whole of this lesson* – and learn the mindset.

Lesson 2

Mock advertising

Before you spend one penny on valuations, surveys and mortgage applications, here's a failsafe way of checking the achievable rent level for yourself that doesn't rely on anyone else's opinion (or indeed for checking rent levels between lengthy tenancies).

Step 1

Once you're certain you know the area well enough to make comparisons, find out which local paper covering the area that you're interested in has the largest 'Property to Let' section. In major cities, this will probably be a freebie like *Loot*. In other towns, it may well be a local paper with a good track record. Get hold of a couple of weeks' back editions – you'll need at least two to three weeks to make this work.

What are you looking for?

Ideally, find a property that resembles the one that you're interested in and find out what kind of money other landlords are asking for similar sounding units. Buildings that only 'work' when everything's running brilliantly often rely on over tight margins.

Will careful research help reduce the iniquitous voids?

Yes. It's possible to be always full (or as near as makes no difference). In fact it's standard independent's practice. We don't want empty property hanging on for the sake of a marginal rent decrease (see below).

How to calculate using the landlord's 13-month year

Landlords should only ever use weekly rents – if you don't believe me read London's glossies and see how established agents have always advertised. Advertised weekly, a £100 p.w. rent generates £5,200 –

advertised at £400 per month it generates £4,800 – a month less. Set weekly rent and, if tenants want to pay monthly, multiply by 52 and divide by 12.

Rent £100 per week	Property filled 52 weeks	Best annual income £5,200
Rent £100 per week	Property empty 8 weeks	Best annual income £4,400
Rent £95 per week	Property filled 52 weeks	Best annual income £4,940
Rent £90 per week	Property filled 52 weeks	Best annual income £4,680

Step 2

Watch out for the same units advertised week after week. They're too expensive, wrongly located, badly presented – or possibly all three. Holding reasonable quality investment property that doesn't shift quickly means you'll need to tweak something.

Step 3

With perseverance, you'll find similar properties at similar rents. If similar properties are cheaper – adjust your expectations now.

Are they advertised once or twice then disappear? Excellent. That means that they are probably let. But don't assume that. Call or email the landlord and ask. Pretend to be a tenant or be honest. Every independent landlord's favourite three words are: 'sorry, it's taken'.

If you've honed those people skills, you might try engaging the landlord in a chat. Where exactly is this building of theirs, etc? Play it by ear.

Step 4

By fair means (or foul) find a way of getting hold of the address of comparable properties. Landlords sometimes have to be quite creative about how they research. Address in hand – visit.

What to look for

Look for 'points in common' with the building that interests you. Adjust your rental expectations up or down accordingly. Better bus routes here? Adjust the rental expectation down. A bit scruffier than your proposal? – adjust up again. This sounds like a lot of palaver, but it isn't really. These things take an odd half hour but they're vitally important for what is a huge investment risk.

Appraise *honestly* whether similar buildings match your expectations. If yours has more plus points, you may be able to ask for a bit more rent, or vice versa. Rental valuation is a fairly imprecise business, despite what agents say.

How effective is this?

Small tweaks to rent can make an enormous difference to demand. Get rent levels too high and you're in for a rough old ride. Get them too low and you'll lose money. Get them right and you're ready to rock and roll.

The downside of knowing the reality

Once you've seen similar properties some of you may find that your hopes have been dashed. Perhaps you need to change tack a bit. Maybe a few streets can make the difference you need. Should you choose a different type of property?

Forget what you've read – landlords with modest portfolios start tearing their hair out when voids take hold.

The upside of knowing the reality

If you've managed to find a good match and have confidence your sums are about right, you'll want to move forward.

Step 5

Place a mock advert. That's right – advertise a building that you haven't even bought yet for the rent you're hoping to achieve. The car industry has done it for years but call it 'Ghost Ads'. Advertise before you pay a penny for fees or surveys. This is the only way to sidestep the hype. (For details on how to word advertisements see Lesson 6: Advertising.)

And then wait to see if the phone rings.

How many calls should a single advert generate?

Take it from me – each unit will take several interested callers per advert. I'm finding that I regularly need two or three viewings – and three viewings means at least five calls because not everyone who calls will be interested or suitable.

Oh and by the way, *don't* include agents who call up in response to your advert, they don't count but they *do* call – all the time. Ignore them. You're tallying genuine tenants who are actually looking to rent somewhere right now.

Now this suggestion always makes novices blanch – but it works. Every time. And before you start panicking about what to say to callers I've already told you the independent landlord's favourite phrase: 'sorry, it's taken'.

Don't pay out a penny until you've had chance to advertise twice and had a fair response *both* times.

Lesson 3

Yields

Let's start by committing a modern heresy. No reputable economist would use the term 'yield' to express the financial viability on *any* residential property investment. It's simply not an accurate enough term to cover the breadth of returns or potential losses on such a complex, long-term investment.

But why should I care about such nit-picky technicalities, or the answers?

- Because the devil's in the detail in this game.
- Because you owe it to yourself not to let some simplistic headline figure be tapped out on a calculator by an agent or broker with axes to grind – particularly if you're going to borrow money.

What you need is some understanding of the various returns that residential property offers – their pitfalls and advantages.

The difference between yield and return

First we need to break down the two financial rewards that can be available to investment landlords.

- *Yield* is the day-to-day cash received from an asset – like rent.
- *Return* is the total gain (however received, through rent surpluses and capital appreciation, etc.) expressed as a proportion of the purchase price. This means that the return will *include* the yield but not necessarily be the same figure.

Yield as a way to express investment returns is best used for assets that are:

1. Highly liquid.
2. Easily tradable.
3. Have low transaction costs (the costs of buying and disposing).
4. Where there's little movement between purchase and sale prices.

Now, does this sound like the UK property market? I think not.

Yield is an incomplete measurement

Yield is a snapshot of, rather than the whole picture. An easy answer for agents with calculators. What's more, as a replacement for a standard profit and loss calculation that reflects individual finances, its appropriateness diminishes.

Why the term causes such confusion

Originally, yield was designed to show the relationship between *capital* invested in certain types of investments and the likely annual return (which is what agents are trying to tell you, albeit somewhat inaccurately). This is virtually impossible with property, especially residential property where borrowings and different investment ratios are in play. (For those of you wanting a worthwhile equation, see the end of this lesson.)

The commodity aspect that no one mentions

What property investment does offer is a decent commodity aspect, not often available to straightforward armchair investors. Put simply, housing remains a commodity in *permanent demand*. So long as tenants, supply and costs remain broadly in balance you should never run out of customers, whereas commercial prices and rents depend on economic performance (positive or negative).

Why borrowers with no repayment strategy are asking for trouble

Borrowers with no repayment strategy are playing a risky returns game, based on the myth of permanently soaring prices. With any other form of investment (or, bluntly, gambling with borrowed money) lenders would be slamming their doors.

Why yield alone is so incomplete

Residential property begins, rather than ends with the initial investment. Unlike a shares portfolio that you simply buy, watch and do nothing bar trade periodically, rental property requires you to do something all the time – or pay someone else to do that something. It's a working investment requiring time and effort. It isn't a straightforward 'investment' at all.

Farming isn't a bad analogy

Growing crops produces a commodity. And so does owning a property, where rent is the product. Let's imagine potatoes are the commodity crop. The market price includes seed, insecticide, mainly labour and somewhere in the fraction of a kilo on the supermarket shelf, the land price itself. The complete return for the farmer is not simply profit on his potatoes but also includes the rising land values of being good at what he does. He may take a risk, perhaps investing in asparagus crowns. Higher crop price feeds through to an increase in the value of the land. Yield is that year's profit. Return is the complete financial benefit. Of course, not every farmer has the right conditions to grow asparagus. Location and climate are key. Besides, if everyone grew asparagus, there'd soon be a glut and prices would start to fall – along with the price of his land. Starting to see any similarities yet?

All investment relies on faith in the market

Plus, the investment side of residential property is starkly different from the commodity side of housing. Investments rely on faith. On a shared belief that certain items will retain or increase its current value (think, gold, stocks and shares, etc). Their value is also underpinned by a shared belief that the value of the purchase is likely to hold or potentially increase in value. The higher the likely increase, the higher the risk taken – and the further to fall if you miscalculate.

Investment landlords who've been in the market for decades don't need telling that no market is more sustained by faith than UK property. Consumers are conditioned to expect year on year growth and complain of slumps when annual price increases so much as stall. Far too many landlords are dependent on rising value to bail them out of promiscuous borrowings.

Overall return is what really matters to private landlords

The overall return is what matters to any investor, including landlords. Those of you lucky enough to have been advised by *genuine* professionals, Chartered Surveyors (RICS), Architects (RIBA), Accountants (ACCA) or others with years of study supporting their opinions, will probably be aware of the full financial implications of property investments. Others with no more than agents or journalists to quote fat-sounding figures may not be so well prepared. Beyond the initial purchase, landlords pay down their *capital* while retaining their rental (usually increasing) income stream, meaning the two factors used to calculate yields continue moving apart.

Why yields appear to rise and fall

By now you'll see that soaring property prices combined with stable rents will inevitably make yields fall. Just as falling prices make yield soar. That doesn't mean that investors who can crunch their own numbers can't find an investment which will make money. The real sums you need to get to grips with are costs out and rent in. Pretty simple, really.

How to do a simple yield calculation

Nevertheless, because they're used so commonly, it's best to know how the yield calculations in play are calculated by agents. Let's take a property with a notional value of £100,000.

Assume a rent £10,000 per year. Divide the annual rental income by the capital outlay and the 'yield' becomes 10 per cent.

So, the exact same property, which has increased in value to say, £200,000 with the same assumed rent of £10,000 shows a yield of only 5 per cent.

Mmmm.

Another scenario – the same property, falling in property price from your original £100,000 investment to say £75,000 with the same annual rent of £10,000. Your yield just shot up to 13 per cent.

Oh?

Let's calculate that yield one final time

Purchased a property for £100,000 three or four years ago? Then watched its price skyrocket to over £250,000? Your yield has been slashed to a lamentable 4 per cent. But haven't you made a packet overall – even after the taxman's take?

Simple profit and loss accounts always show a truer individual picture

Everyone's circumstances vary. How much they borrowed (or didn't) from whom and at what rate. The *only* thing that matters is what a particular property will yield to you. It's called profit in old-fashioned parlance.

Learn how to factor in the true purchase costs

Using the same figures as before, let's borrow £100,000. And let's keep that loan running for 20 years. Then sell that building for, say, £250,000 and cash in. Because your interest payments are probably tax deductible – you'll be charged Capital Gains Tax on the whole £150,000 profit (minus allowances and tapering, etc). However, you'll have *paid out* at least £200,000 for that building once mortgage payments are included – tax relief didn't *exempt* you from all interest. Give away thousands in fees and don't keep generating maximum rent – then ask yourself how much you *really* made.

For the average landlord with a modest portfolio

Yield is thus reduced from something to rely on, to something worth throwing into the consideration pot. What the expressed yield can *never* be in the volatile UK housing market is a single good enough reason to buy any particular building unless everything else makes financial sense in your circumstances.

$$\text{Yield} = \frac{\text{cash received in a given period}}{\text{purchase price paid}}$$

Here's how to do a couple of more worthwhile calculations. Don't forget to divide each result by the number of years you've held the asset to produce an accurate *annual figure*.

$$\text{Return} = \frac{\text{capital appreciation} + \text{yield } \textit{minus} \text{ all costs/fees} + \text{labour} + \text{time}}{\text{purchase price paid}}$$

The whys and wherefores

How long did it take you to read this more complex of lessons, 20 minutes? To work out basic agency yield on a calculator? A minute or two? To try the complex calculations? To find the thirteenth month? Maybe a quarter of an hour. Like most aspects of property investment, the practicalities are quick. Will the income cover the outgoings and will there be a profit? If not – are you willing to fund the difference? And from where?

Further information

For further information check the internet. Avoid agency websites and go for the truly independent sites. I'd recommend a browse through *www.yourmoney.com* and head for the landlord section. The Royal Institute of Chartered Surveyors website *www.rics.co.uk* has some excellent features on finance. *The Times* and the *Guardian* and the *Daily Mail* have excellent archives on personal finance available online. Or pay a small charge and join the local Small Landlord Association which will give you a person to speak to direct, a monthly circular with loads of updated information plus stacks of freebies.

— CHECKLIST/SUMMARY —

■ Yields can be tricky to apply to the private rental sector.

■ Landlords need to consider the entire return which includes yield.

■ A more worthwhile equation for working out genuine costs is included in the lesson.

■ Landlords are not armchair investors. Once purchased, these investments need to *work* to earn their keep and that's *your* job as the landlord.

■ Property can be a volatile market. Be prepared. Keep a financial float.

■ Yields as calculated by your local lettings agent show falls as property prices rise and vice versa.

▨ Always base your decisions on an income versus outgoings account. Never rely on rough yield sums.

▨ Make sure you crunch your own numbers with ruthless honesty.

▨ Experienced landlords use weekly rents for valuation psychology and slightly higher annual product.

▨ Read the whole of this lesson – not just this checklist.

Lesson 4

Selecting agents

Ah, the agents! Some landlords swear by them. Some landlords swear about them.

Despite recent landlord investment running into billions of pounds, agency services remain effectively accountable to no one.

Who uses managing agents?

A *minority* of all landlords – mainly those new to the business. But far more of us manage very nicely without them. The vast majority of landlords simply won't pay such high costs. Here's a salutary tale.

> ### WARNING ANECDOTE
>
> A half-hour chat in the mid 90s between myself and a manager of one of the South East's more reputable agencies was when I first realised how widespread the misunderstanding about this simple 1988 housing legislation was.
>
> 'How?' he asked, 'was he to solve a problem that had just been unearthed during a court application for possession?'
>
> Not understanding that the Housing Act 1988 was a initially a *two part process* (like a decree nisi and a decree absolute) – which *required* service of a 'Prior Notice of the creation of an assured shorthold tenancy' to be signed by the tenant *before* a valid shorthold could be established – his agency had been operating by issuing only the second stage paperwork.
>
> The judge had correctly explained that because no Prior Notice had been signed by tenants, their leases were *not 'shortholds'* at all – but straightforward 'assured leases' with no guaranteed 'rights of repossession' and – unless a tenant breached some term of their lease – indefinite. A nightmare of indescribable proportions for

trusting investors. This agency had hundreds of leases called one thing but which in law, were quite another.

All the benefits of shortholds had been tossed away because the agency hadn't done its homework – despite charging top whack! And despite being a paid up member of one of the largest, much vaunted lettings associations.

What could I say?

In fact – landlords and agents all over England and Wales got themselves into such a mess over this simple one page Notice that in the late 90s the Government changed the default position of the legislation (you'll be glad to read). Now, unless a tenant can produce written evidence from the landlord/agent that they are being offered an 'assured' lease – every lease signed is automatically a 'shorthold' – even unwritten leases are shortholds without proof otherwise (unless the tenancy falls outside the scope of the legislation – see Lesson 5: Assured shorthold leases).

It's one thing making a mess oneself – quite another to pay someone to so spectacularly do it for you!

So, where was I – before I made your hair stand on end? Ah, yes. So, despite only servicing a fraction of the nation's rentals, agents make all that money from a minority of investors.

Should landlords use agents or not?

That's a personal choice. Personally, I cannot see the logic in paying for what are simple tasks that take a matter of hours a year to manage. Most landlords prefer to retain both the profit and control.

Why do some landlords use agents?

Usually it's nervousness and a lack of information about what's actually involved. But this knowledge gap is costly. It is cheaper to read a guide or join a small landlords association and learn the ropes.

Why do agents charge so much?

Because they can.

But don't agents offer guarantees?

Organising a system that protects the tenant's deposit or maybe the landlord's rent from outright fraud and offering access to expensive 'rent guarantee schemes' that generate them extra commission just isn't a sufficient improvement in trading conduct to justify their costs, I'm sorry to say. Besides which, much of this 'guarantee' is superseded by the 2007 legislation on deposits anyway.

What's the best way to manage my agent then?

All I can say with confidence is that landlords who know what they are doing *first* then employ an agent to do it on their behalf *second*, will always be better prepared to tackle some of the worst excesses of some lettings agents. Here's a flavour of the trade.

Article One

One of London's *most reputable* agents charged cleaning costs from a tenant's deposit at almost £125 an *hour* (£495 for four man hours to be precise). Then, when the landlord challenged the agents, they promptly offered her a discount – simultaneously refusing to pay it by insisting that the balance of more than £80 was used up completing a tax return they insisted was necessary. For a short let, this agent was charging the landlord a walloping 26 per cent plus VAT. The agency excuse – this is the going rate for the cleaning company they use.

Well, less than eight miles away – my cleaner earns £7 per hour.

Article Two

This is related to a neat landlord scam and can be found in Lesson 9 on selecting tenants, so read on.

So what do I need to know about letting agents to protect my and my tenant's interests?

This lesson is telling you what an agent can offer, ie what they *should do* for their considerable slice of your risk-loaded income, and what they can and often do charge landlords *and tenants*.

The downside to using agencies

Some landlords have tight budgets too and need to weigh up carefully the choices between paying an agency the entire likely monthly difference between rent and costs – or rolling up their own sleeves to save money – sometimes literally. These practical people I refer to as 'independents'. Many tenants simply won't rent through agents because their fees are so high.

How agents can negatively affects tenant's preconceptions of their landlord

Tenants whose only contact with their landlord is via some very expensive office with fancy cars parked outside can draw the wrong conclusion entirely. There's a great deal of psychology involved in good landlord/tenant relationships. That posh office implies (however subconsciously) that you, the landlord, are de facto wealthy, and if the rent is a bit late or infrequent, it won't necessarily matter. Outrageous – of course it is. But don't kid yourself – we all make value judgements every day and tenants are people too.

By way of balance

In all fairness, because tenants are subjected to a great deal of financial sharp practice, some prefer the services of an agent who'll act as an intermediary following a bad landlord experience.

Similarly, some landlords find it almost impossible to strike the right balance with tenants. Either they become too friendly – or they are too autocratic. Neither of these works well, which is why landlords struggling with their tempers can come to such repeated grief. If you really feel incapable of maintaining a reasonable, firm but fair approach, or finding solutions to rent arrears that don't involve shouting, your best bet may well be to use an agent who can offer you the distance that you may well need. But it's cheaper to learn some people skills.

WARNING ANECDOTE

Forget fashion – landlords are in business to make cold hard cash. Until recently, *all* councils and major landlords employed armies of rent collectors. It worked brilliantly. Arrears were very low. Paying rent once a month by direct debit or standing order is a relatively new phenomena brought to the fore by new agencies, who want money to arrive with no effort to maximise profitability. This is brilliant with good tenants but disastrous with bad payers. Many independents still make rent collections because they *work*. Besides, low-cost units – units with sharers and particularly students on low incomes – need hands on management, not some distance version.

Don't tenants resent the landlord turning up?

Not good ones with nothing to hide. Some welcome the monthly or even weekly contact to, say, report minor issues about the unit. Not complaints – just small things like dripping taps – or sometimes more personal issues like a potential conflict with other tenants in the building they'd prefer you dealt with. I couldn't count the Christmas cards I've opened with December's rent tucked inside. For almost 40 years, my mother had to have a driver on the final rent day before Christmas because she always came home tipsy – too many celebratory sherries. Yes it can be like this. It really can.

So, use an agent if you want or need to – but not because you don't know what should be happening.

What types of agency services are out there and where are they?

Agents of every type are *everywhere*. What you decide to purchase depends on your appetite for costs. My *strong advice* is to ask around – before signing up to anything on the high street. And watch yourself for tie-in clauses and up-front fees running into hundreds of pounds with no guarantee of decent service.

WARNING ANECDOTE

Some agents have developed the fairly insidious practice of front loading their entire management fees. Say you have a unit with a weekly rent of £100 – and the agent (at 15 per cent plus VAT) gets a tenant in on a six-month lease. The agent then collects from the tenant between four and six weeks' rent as deposit – let's say £500. Plus a full four weeks' rent in advance – another £400. Now the agent deducts six months' management fees (that's 26 weeks' costs – approximately £520).

Now, you *may* be lucky – they may have chosen a good tenant – but they could have just have let to someone who will never pay another penny. Use agents who run parallel risks with you over rent/management fees.

Examine how your agency service is structured

Lettings agencies tend to have nice front offices with amicable staff on targets who earn commission per rental.

However, the Cinderella service of property management will probably be run in a back office somewhere else (and often many miles away) and be staffed by a completely different group of backroom staff. By splitting their service into commission-driven salespeople and backroom staff, agents have created a mismatch between immediate gain and long-term management. The person anxious to get a name on the lease will *not* be the poor person endlessly on the phone or writing letters, chasing rent, organising endless repairs or worse.

Beware of agents who want contractual consent to repair without your authorisation

Be especially wary of signing any contractual consent, which allows any agent to authorise repairs below a certain fixed value of, say £250. Most agents have in-house and highly profitable sidelines in maintenance and repair and an authority like that can allow them to run up astronomical costs over the course of a year (which always somehow stay below the benchmark £250). This is an unnecessary degree of freedom to decide about what *you* pay out, without some kind of veto. Avoid this term or set a more savvy level of, say, £50.

If you sign up – let them *earn* their fees

Avoid responding to an ongoing stream of unnecessary calls from an agent to whom you're paying full management fees – except for issues that could cost you money. They're being paid to do a job and should get on with it. Here's a good rule of thumb.

If the sink was working perfectly when tenants moved in and it's now blocked – the tenants blocked it and they get the bill.

If, on the other hand, you left them with a washing machine on its last legs that died, that's your bill.

And to quote Lord Denning, 'a tenant must do the little jobs around the place that a reasonable tenant should do' – so don't get stung at top price by the agent's maintenance department for every door handle that needs a screwdriver – or for fuses. And if your agent doesn't know or understand how to apply this most famous legal judgement – how good are they?

Your appetite for costs

Broadly speaking, how much you're prepared to pay for agency services and what type to use is entirely down to your own budget and your aptitude for managing third parties with access to your money.

Rent payment guarantees

Some agents also will try to sell you 'unpaid rent insurance' and call it a 'rent guarantee scheme'. It's really a costly item that landlords with good tenant management simply don't need. The fairly large premiums will eat up *yet another* hefty slice of rent. And, naturally, the agent gets a commission for selling these policies.

Remember no business ever guarantees that everything will run without a hitch. Don't take problems personally. If, frankly, your number crunching is so tight that you can't afford a couple of month's unpaid rent while you get a Possession Order, your margins are squeezed too tight for this business.

Agency contracts – *caveat emptor* (buyer beware!)

As with everything else I've warned you to check thoroughly, read even the most reputable, nationwide agency contracts *very carefully before signing*. You might like to try asking more than one agency for specimen contracts and take them to take home to read. *You* are the customer here – so act the part. *Never* be afraid to negotiate – this is a tough old business.

What to check contracts for

- How long you're committing yourself for.

- How to get out of contracts if no tenants are found.

- The little 'extras' that no one mentions – for example – if your first tenant signs a six-month lease then decides to stay for a year – are the agency going to charge you as well as your tenant for that unnecessary lease extension? If so – why, when a statutory periodic gives the landlord more ready access to possession (see Lesson 5: Assured Shorthold leases)?

- Who gets charged – what if the tenant is not a good choice and needs to be evicted (legal costs are usually extras)?

- Are there set-up fees for landlords as well as tenants?

- Are they re-applied if the unit needs re-letting quickly?

- Do they have a repair fee limit? Ask where your veto starts.

- Ask what proportion of their tenants obtain a full deposit refund.

- Ask how disagreements about damage are managed between landlord and tenant.

- Check out individual tenancy set-up costs – additional charges for leases and fees for lease signing, inventory costs, reference costs and add them all up.

- Make a list of everything you see and take it to your agent to get a price – then file the price list safely.

- Then finally, mark up your personal diary and make sure that, for example, if part of their service includes a quarterly inspection of your tenanted unit and feedback to the landlord, you get what you're paying for.

The list is endless but you get the picture.

What kinds of agencies are there, what kind of money are they charging and what do they actually do?

Broadly, agencies come in three shapes.

Tenant finding services

These agents specialise in just finding tenants. They charge the landlord (and *theoretically* only the landlord, though believe it or not I have, however, heard salutary tales from tenants who've been charged an £80 fee for the privilege of being chauffeured to *view* a property!). But they cost. Near to me a tenant find service alone can charge eight per cent of the entire contract.

These agents should do all the background checks you require. Some will even instruct an independent inventory service for you. Ask about costs to you and the tenant. (For comprehensive advice on how to compile legally binding inventories for nothing see Lesson 7: Inventories.)

These middlemen do not run tenancies but can act as powerful magnets for tenants, especially in large cities. Given that they do their own advertising, you can offset some of the saved advertising costs against what they'll charge. Some will carry out initial viewings and allow landlords an ultimate veto. None should hold tenants' deposits (see Lesson 10: Deposits, for new rules) unless they offer the end of contract services to make this effective.

These services save time/effort on the day-to-day issues of advertising, discussing matters on the phone with prospective tenants and of course, viewings. If you're happy to let someone else choose your tenants for you, or can find someone who'll provide you with referenced options, but are uncomfortable about handing over full management to a third party, this service can be worth exploring.

Tenant find plus management

Cheaper than their more common colleagues of full management, these rarer agencies charge around ten per cent plus VAT of the rent yielded by each contract – and are the *most* likely to snatch a full fee up-front. They should find you a suitable tenant and carry out the necessary background checks. Sometimes they offer a lease of their own. Others take no responsibility and expect you to sign the lease with your tenant – that way *you'll* be liable if you forget to arrange something obligatory like an annual Gas Safety Certificate or if furniture doesn't comply. They should provide an inventory check both in and out (there will be additional charges for this). And they'll often set up the arrangements for rent collection – usually by direct debit via their accounts department. They do not always offer repairs services or 24-hour repair lines, but act more as middlemen (during office hours) between the landlord and tenant; cutting out the hassle on the phone as landlord and tenant blame one another for a problem drain. They may be able to suggest tradespeople to carry out repairs.

Full management services

The Sexy Sadie of them all (in fact you'll be tripping over them on most high streets) and at between 15 and 20 per cent plus VAT they give all the above, plus the following.

- An initial rental valuation (which you should already know).

- Provision of a legally binding lease (available elsewhere for about £2 – see Lesson 5: Assured shorthold leases).

- Rent collection – usually by direct debit.

- Repairs (charged as additions and deducted at source from your rent).

- Inventories (some charge both landlord and tenant).

- Checking your unit to ensure that all statutory regulations are met (see the Lesson 12: The *serious* responsibilities).

- Holding spare keys for emergencies.

Full management should also include routine quarterly inspections of the unit. Agents should notify the utilities and local authorities of who's moving in and out and also take moving in and moving out meter/utilities readings and notifying the companies/authorities appropriately. They should also ensure they have forwarding addresses for tenants to submit final accounts to and should hold onto deposit releases until they are sure the final bills have been settled by the vacating tenant. Final inspections and arrangements for repairs/cleaning – which you can do yourself in little more than one full day in total – spread across a six-month let.

And . . .

Between those things lay a never-ending list of chargeable items for landlords and tenants. Watch this doesn't amount to a regular extra charge for endless small jobs which may quite reasonably have waited until the tenancy ended or could constitute improvements.

Additional services

A decent agent should have the expertise to offer *qualified* advice on:

- Building Regulations.
- Solid information on Houses in Multiple Occupation.
- Consumer protection and legal requirements.
- Fire regulations and furniture requirements.
- General housing law and landlord and tenant legal advice.

But none of the above necessarily fall into the free category. Many agents do engage a qualified RICS surveyor who genuinely is in a position to give you high quality advice on Building Regulations. Some have in-house qualified accountants whose advice you may wish to buy. However, unqualified advice is as much use as a chocolate teapot for Building Regulations, planning, the law or tax because it won't carry legal indemnity for error. Remember my initial advice to move liability, wherever possible to a *recognised* professional.

Deducting your tax at source

Something you need to know is that any managing agent is *legally obliged* to deduct tax from the rents before forwarding the balance to landlords *who reside abroad* and the agent is obliged to ensure these payments reach HMRC. Unbelievably, the same tax law obliges tenants to make similar deductions and forward them where no agency is used.

What's the best way to choose an agent?

I couldn't speculate – it's horses a for courses service. What I do know is that, *were I* selecting an agent – I would *not* hand over control of a massive asset like property without seeing the whites of someone's eyes who is accountable – nor would I settle for a 21 year old, who's only been doing the job six months.

Many agencies are combined sales and lettings options and that *can be* a conflict – and also cloud what the office is really good at. If an office can survive on lettings alone, it's probably doing okay.

Ask if they have written references from satisfied landlords. If not, ask why not. It would be the first thing I'd do – wouldn't you?

Never get fobbed off with half an answer – if the agent's evasive now – things won't improve once your entire rental stream is accessible *only* through his office. Remember – contracts are always easier to get into than out of.

Be realistic about what agents can achieve

Agents cannot (and shouldn't be expected to) replicate what a well prepared independent can offer. And in fairness, if they did try to, some landlords would be screaming down the phone at them ten times a week about unlet property. An agent's position is profitable but not necessarily pleasant. It's unrealistic to expect an agent to prioritise your unit in the way you'd do yourself – agencies are volume players.

What you can really buy

I hate to be the endless killjoy here, but when you start to see how it actually works, ask yourself if this kind of expensive arrangement is really what you want? Remember that the whole purpose of the 1988

Housing Act was to make assured shorthold tenancies trouble-free to set up, simple to run, and with a legal *guarantee of possession* after the first six months. Twenty per cent is an awfully large slice of rent for managing tenants who haven't enough rights to balance on a pinhead after six months.

No one knows better than I how lovely it would be to hand over the odd late calls and the misplaced keys. But is that twice-a-year drama really worth 20 per cent (or your entire realistic profit)? And just how many decisions about a new boiler or carpets do you want to leave with a stranger who gets their hands on your cash first?

On deposits and agents

Full management agents used to hold deposits on behalf of landlords and, in theory, they should consult landlords over deposit returns and retentions and play honest broker.

However, given that almost a hundred million pounds of deposit money is illegally withheld each year, the government has acted. It has finally moved to intervene (in April 2007) to prevent deposit theft with a new compulsory system for *all* landlords and agents.

If your managed unit has repeated tenant or rent payment problems

Start asking yourself what it is about the overall management (of agent or landlord) or the type of unit – or its condition – if you repeatedly attract poor quality tenants. If you (or your agent) are repeatedly attracting the bad *minority* – look closely at the management. Remember that for every rotten tenant there are a dozen brilliant ones, so *if you never get one*, start wondering why?

WARNING ANECDOTE

At a meeting, one local managing agent (part of one of the national chains) admitted to me that more than half their properties did not have a current Gas Safety Certificate. Horrified, I asked how this could possibly have happened. She shrugged. The lettings' staff handed over *all the keys* to the incoming tenants, she explained.

'Not enough training' – her words, not mine. This agent had *no* access *at all* to literally hundreds of units. She couldn't see how to get round this problem.

I made a few practical suggestions and moved to chat to someone with more sense. The new expert lettings agency business can be a very strange beast.

The landlord's clause

Endless discussion about voids can be a useful excuse for sloppy practice. All decent assured shorthold leases contain a clause, which allows landlords (or agents) to undertake viewings during the final month of the tenancy. Independents use this month's notice period to find new tenants. At the right rent level and with good tenant relationships, it's possible to have one tenant move out at noon and another move in at dusk. This gives a six-hour cleaning period and you can do a great deal of wiping in six hours. However, this clearly isn't practicable where redecoration and industrial cleaning are required. But even that should be reasonably organised by an efficient agent within *one week* maximum. Agents refusing to utilise this last month wisely are wasting your money – not theirs!

How can I ensure my agent uses this landlord clause in the lease?

Instruct your agent to notify you as soon as tenants give notice and insist they get moving. *Check up every few days.* Don't be fobbed off. If their phone isn't ringing, they're probably not actively marketing. If not – get on their case. You can't afford weeks of voids. Tenants are not, by and large, stupid people. They can see past a few dishes in the sink.

What if the unit has been allowed to deteriorate beyond the normal untidy state?

Ask why your agent didn't pick this up during a routine quarterly inspection and act earlier to protect your belongings. Or didn't they do what they charged you for in the contract? Insist that staff do explain to prospective tenants that the building will be in the correct condition before they move in. If your agent has pre-tenancy photos of how the unit will be presented – so much the better. If not, why not? I certainly always take them as insurance for disputes, as does every independent I know these days (see Lesson 7: Inventories). Make your agent learn how to be flexible. There's always more than the way they've always done things to improve results.

A final caution

When challenged about their astonishing fees, a spokesperson for ARLA told a BBC reporter that costs were so high because it may take 30 viewings to let a unit. I could weep when I hear things like this. There's something terribly wrong with either the unit or the rent level when 30 people have turned it down.

I repeat – decent units with rents set that reflect the local levels of supply and demand should let out relatively easily (two, three, four viewings maximum, before you have to start worrying and doing something like dropping the rent or buying a new sofa to make your unit more obviously appealing).

If you engage an agent make *them* work *for you* not the other way round. Landlords who sound as if they know what they are doing will always get better service than those who don't.

In conclusion

It needs to be remembered that the land of the lettings agent remains a quicksand for the unwary. There is no guarantee you won't be charged over and over for a service done once and there's precious little comeback with teeth. Moreover, this whole agency 'ah well, it takes time to rent a unit' philosophy is alien to an independent landlord whose day-to-day losses are a cold, hard reality.

Whys and wherefores

Agency practice is so varied, there's no reading list I can suggest. Weigh up the services and the costs of each service provider you find and try negotiating. The internet will provide thousands of hits for UK lettings agents. Press archives will let you access the numerous articles that are repeatedly written by concerned journalists. And, if you contact some of their trading associations ARLA/NAEA etc direct, they'll send you enough information to fill a skip. I'm afraid that this is the one lesson where each and every landlord is working blind – unless you've been lucky enough to get an agent recommended by a satisfied private landlord.

— CHECKLIST/SUMMARY —

- Genuine professions demand years of scrutinised study (usually at university), challenging levels of examination and ultimate registration with a professional body. No lettings agency can properly call itself 'professional' – they belong to trading associations. Take this up with your MP. Assets this valuable ought to have both an appropriate qualification and a powerful *regulator*.

- Some agencies charge landlords 'front loaded fees'. Don't accept this – find an agent willing to share your risk.

- Check the rate you're committing yourself to pay and make sure there's no tie-in for unduly long periods at this rate.

- If the same tenant stays in place for longer than the initial six-month fixed term, ask the following questions:

  1. Why are the agents renewing the lease rather than offering to let the existing lease run on into a statutory periodic, which offers the maximum advantage to landlords (read Lesson 5: Assured Shorthold leases)?
  2. How much are they charging you and your tenants for the privilege of a lease extension?

- It's the agent's job to make as much money as possible from your investment risk. Understand this. Watch costs don't escalate disproportionately.

- Understand what you sign.

- Agents charge tenants astronomical fees for their services. Be aware that many decent tenants avoid renting through them for this reason.

- Monitor your agent's conduct by asking for regular written reports, etc.

- Agents who do misbehave should always be reported – try Trading Standards.

- If you agree to pay them, let them do their job – don't endlessly interfere.

- Read the whole lesson – even if it's setting your teeth on edge.

Lesson 5

Assured shorthold leases

I need to make something crystal clear here. I am discussing *assured shorthold tenancies only* in this guide. I suggest that no landlord should seriously consider using anything else and should tailor their investments accordingly.

However, some tenancies *cannot* be run as assured shortholds. Landlords considering running any of the exceptions listed below *must* seek alternative advice.

Exceptions

▨ Tenancies which were agreed or began before 15 January 1989.

▨ **Any tenancy where the rent exceeds £25,000 per annum (approximately £500 per week).**

Assured shortholds remain the only tenancies where landlords are protected by *guaranteed 'no fault'* repossession. To be valid, assured shortholds must comply with all the legal criteria. Many landlords whose rent exceeds £480 per week (irrespective of what the lease calls itself) fall outside the benefits of this legislation and should seek advice about other methods of gaining repossession.

▨ Any tenancy where the rent is £250 per year or less (Greater London £1,000 per year).

▨ A business tenancy or one where a licence to consume alcohol is bought/sold.

▨ A tenancy let with more than two acres of land.

▨ The tenancy of an agricultural holding.

▨ A tenancy granted to a student by an educational body (ie a university).

■ A holiday let.

■ Letting by a resident landlord.

■ There are some other very limited exceptions where tenancies were previously assured tenancies, where pre-1989 tenancies have been succeeded on the death of a tenant, where secure tenancies from local authorities change hands or on the expiry of long leaseholds.

Background on assured shorthold tenancies

When these shorthold leases were created back in 1988, they offered some revolutionary advantages for landlords, explained elsewhere. However, tenants were also given a modicum of security of tenure, where, during the initial fixed term it is more difficult to obtain possession unless the tenant is misbehaving. This short period of protection is called the initial fixed term.

What's an initial fixed term?

Initially, the shortest time landlords could offer an assured shorthold lease was six months. After this six months has expired, any landlord can apply to the court (see Lesson 11: Ending tenancies) which has no option but to grant possession to the landlord/agent. No legal reason is required – that's the whole nub of shortholds – landlords can choose to terminate them at any time after the initial fixed term has expired by giving two months' written notice beforehand.

And if that doesn't seem like much of a deal – here's another anecdote to give you a flavour of the good old days.

WARNING ANECDOTE
Back in the early 80s, a good tenant's recommendation was about as much as a landlord could reasonably hope for. So when Annie – a good tenant – recommended her friend Mr Jenson we'd no reason to worry. What, unfortunately, Annie *didn't* know was that Mr Jenson had been successfully recovering from alcoholism and he relapsed soon after moving in.

For more than 11 years Mr Jenson made nonsense of any notion of landlord control and deployed with skill every legal right he enjoyed to secure his own tenancy. Though he was harmless, female tenants were unnerved by having to clamber over him when he was drunk and incapable on the stairs. His habit of trying to dispose of potato peelings down the toilet resulted in repeated drenching by foul water of the downstairs flat's bedroom. Rent payment was erratic and he ran up considerable arrears. Eventually, after a particularly bad event, we decided to try the courts. Our solicitor had advised us to continue accepting housing benefit cheques during the long wait for court, so we did. We got 'our day' in court. After ten minutes the judge intervened. In accepting rent after serving Notice we'd set up a whole new tenancy. No case. Mr Jenson went back to the flat victorious – got drunk and the police were called – who promptly smashed in both the main door and the flat door leaving us with their bills too. This nonsense went on for six more long years before Mr Jenson finally was admitted to hospital where he died, sad and alone. We can only thank God he didn't exercise his *legal right* to leave his tenancy in his will to his son, who was then in prison for rape. The 1974 Housing Act gave absolutely unbelievable powers and rights to tenants, which many are still exercising today.

Now that's why experienced landlords still celebrate shortholds. So, if six months and a few weeks hassle to get a Possession Order seems harsh – remember Mr Jenson.

How long does the initial fixed term have to be?

The original minimum set out by the 1988 Housing Act was six months.

However, in 1997, the government tweaked the legislation a bit and it became possible for tenancies of less than six months to be offered as assured shortholds. However, what the government never changed was the tenant's *six-month* period of security of tenure. Ooops.

We have therefore a conundrum. Legitimate leases can be signed for, say, three months...however...the landlord's guarantee of Possession still does *not* start until at least six months has expired. Now, to me at least, the prospect of signing a legally binding lease of *three* months where I cannot get a guaranteed possession for *six*, throws many of the advantages of the original legislation into the trash.

Experienced landlords always *offer a six-month initial fixed term to a complete stranger*

It is my *strong advice* therefore that *all* landlords offer assured shorthold leases with an initial fixed term of six months only. That way, your tenant is obliged to keep all the terms of the lease (especially including payment of rent) for as long as they enjoy security of tenure. You are tied to one another which is fair and simple. Go for the straightforward option every time. Don't ever throw an unnecessary spanner into the works or let agents persuade you to do so.

Why longer initial fixed terms can be problematic

Don't offer (or allow agents to offer) one-year leases willy-nilly. One-year leases give an initial fixed term of *one whole year* and your new tenant (a stranger until yesterday) enjoys security of tenure for a year, rather than six months.

Two broad types of leases (for independent landlords)

Off the peg leases

These leases are supplied by a variety of organisations and cost between £2 and £5 each depending on the number you order. My personal choice supplier of everything for landlord and tenant remains Oyez (their phone number is given at the end of lesson), which supplies nationwide and whose leases have to be legally up to date. In addition, Oyez leases are the product of a year's negotiation with the Office of Fair Trading and are fair under UK contract law. Off the peg leases like these are four pages long and cover pretty much everything it is reasonable for a landlord or tenant to demand of one another and remain within the Housing Act. (Other suppliers you might like to check out are the Small Landlords Associations, Residential Landlords Association and many other stationers and online lease suppliers who all charge a few pounds each.)

Tailor-made leases

These leases can be obtained from local solicitors everywhere. They can work well but need regular review because the law can change. This can be a costly business for landlords. Solicitor's charges will usually be around £100 and you'll have an annual bill to make sure your lease remains up to date. Tailor-made leases can also be unduly long. I've seen leases for a six-month let that run to 30 pages of close type – which daunts tenants.

How difficult are leases to fill in?

They aren't. Overleaf are the questions on a typical off-the-peg lease. What is essential to remember is that you will need *two leases* for each tenancy – one for your tenant to keep, one for you to keep – both identically completed.

For the purpose of this exercise, I'm looking broadly at the terms contained in an off-the-peg lease, see example on page 66.

One important exception

By now, having read this much of the guide you'll be beginning to understand the ramifications of the new Houses in Multiple Occupation (HMO) legislation. If you're at all confused, you should read the whole of Lesson 13 before continuing because here's another emerging *major* issue for all landlords. At present all decent leases contain a subletting clause, precluding tenants from inviting in other people to help pay the rent. There's often another clause that states that reasonable requests to allow this *should be* agreed by the landlord. Under the new HMO regulations which came into force in April 2006, any unit with more than two individual tenants (or singletons who don't constitute a family unit) may well be classified as an HMO. This means a very substantial risk of reclassification (along with all the subsequent potential safety cost implications) may arise if your couple (or two girls) decide to rent out the spare room and turn a perfectly safe two-bedroom flat let to two individuals into an HMO.

Therefore, having recently taken legal advice myself, I have decided to insert new clauses into one of the blank spaces always provided

Date.......................
(Landlords fill in today's date.)

The Tenant ....
(Landlords fill in the full name of tenant.)

The Landlord ....
(Landlords fill in their own full name.)

Property ....
....
(Landlords fill in the address of the rental unit.)

Term ....
*(Landlords will here see a sentence similar to this: A fixed term of [landlords write six months here]. **Then carefully scribble out the option years.**)*

Start date..................
(Landlords fill out the first date of the tenancy [which may be different to the actual date you're signing the lease].)

Rent.......................
(Fill in the weekly rent – say £100 per week.)

Payable in advance by equal...
(Write weekly/monthly (whichever you decide).)

Payments on the ....
(Write Mondays or 1st day of the month – or every four weeks – whatever you've agreed with your tenant.)

First payment to be made on...
(Write the date you first accept rent (not a cheque – cleared funds only). Ask for cash – or sign leases after a cheque has cleared into your account. Don't sign leases on an uncleared cheque.)

Landlord's address...
(Must be provided.)

....	....	....	....
Landlord's signature	*Date*	*Tenant's signature*	*Date*
....	....	....	....
Witness's signature	*Date*	*Witness's signature*	*Date*

Tenancy agreement for letting a (furnished/unfurnished) dwelling house on an assured shorthold tenancy under Part 1 of the Housing Act 1988 (shown below for *guidance* only – do not replicate without specific legal advice). All landlords should take fairly urgent legal advice on this matter and make sure they keep abreast of this situation. Of course, the courts may decide that withholding this subletting consent is not fair and may, in time, invalidate my clauses. Until then, I intend to insert in the blank space between Parts 4 and 5 of the off-the-peg variety of leases, the following:

> 10 (c) *'It is agreed that it shall be reasonable for the landlord to withhold its consent to any subletting or parting with possession by the tenant or tenants if the subletting or parting with possession (whether in conjunction with any other subletting or parting with possession that the landlord be requested to determine the reasonableness of) results in the creation of a "House in Multiple Occupation" within the meaning of the 2004 Housing Act.'*

> 10(d) *'The tenant shall indemnify the landlord for all costs claims demands liabilities and expenses which the landlord may suffer or incur arising from a breach by the tenant of its obligations under this Agreement.'*

And having read that, you may now begin to see why so many of us prefer the broad sweeping clauses in, say, an Oyez lease.

Confusion relating to fixed terms

During the initial fixed term the tenant is obliged to pay rent. They cannot just move on and abandon their rent liabilities.

Shortly before the end of the six-month fixed term the tenant is free to give one month's written notice. A little earlier (remember the landlords needs to write two months in advance) the landlord is free to give written notice. But neither have to do any such thing. If both parties are happy, these original leases can simply run on with no more paperwork. Simply by the offering and the receiving of rent, your original lease changes into a nifty thing called a statutory periodic tenancy without lifting a finger.

What is a statutory periodic tenancy?

Statutory periodic tenancies are brilliant things that can run for years – all on the original documents – and way beyond any fixed-term periods of tenant security. Their advantage is that they can be concluded fast – by either party. And it's always in the landlord's interest to be closest to the point when they can go for possession. There's absolutely *no need* to offer up a whole new lease and a new fixed term the minute the old one runs out. Find out all about them in the Office of the Deputy Prime Minister's booklet. Call 0870 1226 236 and ask for one, the product code is 97 HC 228B (they're free). Show one to your agent if they always offer lease renewals and charge you and your tenant for the privilege.

When is a lease an assured shorthold lease and how easy is it to set up?

From 1997 onwards, every lease unless it falls into an exceptions category (including unwritten ones) is an assured shorthold – unless tenants can provide written evidence in addition to the lease (which they can't unless you send them a letter specifically saying this *won't* be a shorthold, which is pretty hard to do accidentally – so it won't happen).

Here's a short question and answer session that should help answer most issues.

Questions and answers about leases and licences

Q **What's a shorthold assured lease?**
A It's a contract drawn up between landlord and tenant setting out the broad framework of the agreement between them.

Q **Are leases difficult to understand?**
A Not at all – unless you or your solicitor or agent goes out of their way to make them totally impenetrable. The legal requirements of the 1988 Housing Act are extremely simple.

Q **What do off-the-peg leases cover?**
A The broad issues that need to be mutually agreed between landlord and tenant shown earlier.

Q Is it wise to let someone into a unit without a written lease?

A Absolutely not. In the first instance, you won't be able to apply for accelerated possession without a written contract (see Lesson 11: Ending tenancies). Protect yourself with a lease with *clear* terms to avoid misunderstandings.

Q Where can I obtain leases?

A You have two options.

1. You can approach a solicitor and ask them to draw up a tailor-made lease. For highly specialist units, or where landlords want to make very particular conditions, you'll need a tailor made lease. But remember, your lease can't offer you more rights than the 1988 Act, however nifty you try being!

2. You can buy an off-the-peg lease from any legal stationers such as *www.oyezstraker.co.uk*, large stationers like WH Smith or many online sites such as *www.rla.co.uk*. For the overwhelming majority of tenancies, a straightforward, off-the-peg lease is an efficient, cost-effective tool.

Q Do either kinds have specific advantages or disadvantages?

A The broad sweeping clauses of off-the-peg leases are designed by legal experts who know exactly what they're doing. Of course, you can specify much more detail in a tailor-made lease – but it's over-egging the pudding. In most cases, high specification units need very comprehensive inventories and schedules – but the lease terms are set out by the Housing Acts – and they're already in an off-the-peg lease.

Ill-conceived clauses are more trouble than they're worth. A common one early on that caused problems was that tenants had to clean curtains and carpets before vacation. Have you any idea how dry clean only curtains come out of a hot wash cycle? Off-the-peg leases soon dropped unnecessary clauses.

Q But my agent tells me that I need a specific lease and this will cost a great deal of money to draw up by his firm and have signed.

A Agents say this all the time. I suggest that landlords hearing this should read the handy *free* booklet I told you about earlier and draw their own conclusion – because no arrangement of words changes the Housing Acts. (Call 0870 1226 236 and ask for one, the product code is 97 HC 228B.)

A little about assured shorthold leases

Assured shortholds are simple, effective, and enforceable. Tenants have no security of tenure at all, once the initial fixed term written on the lease has expired (though of course a court process must be gone through to remove the roof from over anyone's head – see Lesson 11: Ending tenancies). Although UK landlord and tenant legislation is immense, by using 1988 assured shortholds, landlords are able to utilise a tiny core of legislation, unaffected by much beyond a few temporary tenant rights.

A few more questions

Q **My agent insists that I offer my property on a minimum one–year let. Does this mean I can't apply for no fault possession for a minimum of a year, sooner than the minimum six months allowed by the legislation?**
A Yes. Insist on an initial lease of six months.

Q **Does that *really* matter?**
A It might, especially if they put an awful tenant in place and you're not guaranteed possession for a whole year.

Q **Why do agents sometimes insist on offering contracts that are longer than the minimum exposure for landlords?**
A That's a very good question. However, experienced landlords always test tenants over the minimum six months. Don't let third parties bully you into the best option for them. Insist on the best option for you (and often tenants too).

Q **What are the options if my tenant *wants to stay longer than the six months* he originally signed a lease for?**
A You can both choose between either of the following options:

　1. Both landlord and tenant can agree to sign another new lease for a further six months. (However creating a whole new lease

means offering the tenant a further minimum fixed term of another six months.)

2. Or, as explained earlier, you may prefer to do nothing at all. Leave the existing paperwork in place and the tenancy automatically converts itself into a statutory periodic tenancy. This retains all the advantages of the original contract. The fixed term has already expired so landlords can give two months' written notice at any time. Tenants again recover the freedom to give a single month's notice, without nailing themselves into a commitment for a full six months' rental liability. This statutory periodic is an underused and excellent arrangement, where agents are left playing gooseberry because unless they *do* something, they can't make charges.

But it works. And tens of thousands of tenancies run on for years in this way, with landlords and tenants discussing matters like rent increases between themselves to great benefit. (Rent increases under this arrangement are explained later in this Q&A section.)

Q Are there any other types of assured shorthold I need to know about?

A Just the contractual periodic, which runs on a month-by-month basis. Again, no fault possession cannot be sought from a court until the first six months has run its course, and, because the periodic runs from one payment to the next, tenants can't be charged rent for the remainder of a period which hasn't been fixed, which raises even more issues. By and large, contractual periodic tenancies don't offer landlords as many advantages as good old assured shortholds with an initial fixed term of six months.

Q Anything else I should consider?

A Yes. Here are a couple that you may not realise (beyond the earlier exemptions):

1. Tenancies can't be created legally with anyone under 18 years of age.

2. Landlords can't legally charge rent unless they divulge their address to the tenant.

Q What about rent increases?

A Rent increases can't occur unless you have a clause in the existing lease that allows them. Off the peg leases don't have them because these days most tenancies don't last long enough for rent hikes.

The solution is very simple. If you propose a rent increase in any tenancy that lasts long enough to become a statutory periodic tenancy and rent increases aren't mentioned in the original lease, you can *ask for* a rent increase by sending a rent increase form to your tenant one month before you want a higher rent. There is a special form for this, called 'Landlord's notice proposing a new rent under an Assured Periodic Tenancy of premises situated in England'. These forms cost around £1 each – and are available from Oyez (or others) as already discussed.

Or you can offer your tenant a whole new lease (with a further fixed term) at a higher rent level – but they're under no obligation to accept it. This can be a fine balancing act between keeping a good quality *known* tenant in place – or risking a newcomer with all that may bring for the sake of a small hike in rent.

Q What if my tenant doesn't agree to a rent increase?

A If your tenant refuses, you can both agree to go your separate ways and one or the other gives notice. However, a good tenant on a slightly lower rent may be much more valuable than an unknown quantity sometime in the future. It's your choice.

Q Anything else I need to understand?

A Yes. In return for all that money and all those restrictions and obligations, tenants buy the 'right to quiet enjoyment' and you are obliged to give them that. Don't interrupt their lives at all except on the very rare occasions that can arise, when landlords genuinely believe that their tenants are not keeping their side of the bargain. Beyond that all landlords wanting to enter their unit once it is let are obliged to give their tenant 24 hours' written notice of their intention to enter and should have a legitimate reason like a repair or quarterly inspection.

A final few questions (these are more specifically for sharers who have joint and several liability leases, ie more than a single tenant in a unit).

Q How many leases do I need for four sharers?
A One lease for the landlord, *one* lease for all the sharers combined – all four signatures plus the landlord's must be in place on both these leases and all must be witnessed and dated. This constitutes *joint and several liability*. In this arrangement, each sharer is liable for their own share of the rent but must make up shortfalls if someone moves out or doesn't pay up. All four signatures must be on the inventory and schedule of condition but each tenant must complete their own individual Tenant's Application Form and Parental Guarantor Form if they're young. (Format available in Lesson 9: Selecting tenants and tying up the deal.)

Leave them with *one* original lease and you keep the other. You may also need a licence from the local authority due to new legislation in force from April 2006 – four sharers is definitely an HMO.

Q What if I want three tenants but they're not friends and I arrange each tenancy separately by advertising a house share?
A Then you'll need six leases and strong nerves for a notoriously complex tenancy like this – one for you and one for each tenant of the three separate tenancies. Each will have its own start date, and its own fixed term – meaning the end point of these tenancies will not necessarily match up. In these cases, each party will be contracted to pay their share of the rent and won't be liable for any shortfall if another party leaves the building. These circumstances will require two leases *per tenancy* and one each of every other form. Again, you may well need a licence (because of new legislation) – three sharers is probably an HMO, which may need licensing.

Q What about letting to a family?
A Here you'd have one lease for the family, one for the landlord – with both adults named and both parties signing one inventory, etc. In some cases, you'd ask for both parents to fill in a Tenant's Application Form, in others, where say only one parent works outside the home, one may suffice.

Q What about this converted house of mine? It has six self-contained units.

A Where any self-contained unit is let, each requires its own individual tenancy arrangements. But beware. With a single property, used by multiple tenants – especially if the conversion occurred before the 1992 Building Regulations – you're probably operating an HMO (see Lesson 13: Houses in Multiple Occupation).

Why do I need to know any of this if I'm using an agent?

Whether or not you use an agent – this is information you *need* to understand. Otherwise, you'll struggle to manage your agent. Knowledge is a win-win situation because information is always king.

Licences (these are different forms of occupancy altogether)

These don't apply for the overwhelming majority of landlords and tenants. They apply where resident landlords invite people into their homes to live and charge rent and where the tenant doesn't enjoy exclusive use of any part of the building. Usually resident landlords provide other services, such as cleaning or meals. Where tenants have almost no security of tenure with an assured shorthold lease, with a licence they have, in effect, none. Landlords charge rents weekly and tenants (or lodgers as they're more commonly known) can be given a week's notice to leave at any time and for no reason. These are historically precarious arrangements for tenants, but many work surprisingly well.

But don't try pretending you're a resident landlord where you live in one flat and a tenant rents another self-contained unit from you upstairs. It won't hold up in court. Nor does the scam of owning large buildings, converted into scrappy bed sits where the landlord pops by each week to leave bread and eggs in the kitchen but lives in a lovely safe house just up the hill. Buildings in multiple occupation are complex to set up and require more than the ingredients for a bread and butter pudding to substantiate.

Leases – options and considerations

Getting started

However simple to understand, leases are very important documents. Responsible landlords need paperwork. So get yourself a paper trail and look after it.

The importance of a Tenant Application Form

(For a suggested format, see Lesson 9: Selecting tenants and tying up the deal.)

A Tenant Application Form can be drawn up by any landlord and has the legal benefit of ensuring the tenant has declared their true identity, previous addresses, employment history, income status (if required), accurate bank details, their National Insurance number or passport number and at least the previous three years' addresses. There's a standard format for you to copy in Lesson 9 because you certainly don't need a solicitor to create these simple forms (for referees and guarantor form details see Lesson 9 on selecting tenants).

The advantage of a Tenant Application Form cannot be overstated. Ground 17 of the 1996 Housing Act makes the making of a deliberate false statement an offence and a completed Tenant Application Form gives written and provable *discretionary grounds for possession*, should you be unlucky enough to find yourself housing a professional fraudster.

To make the tenancy as watertight as possible, a Tenant Application Form might be well joined by a Parental Guarantor Form – for younger tenants these are an absolute *must* and you'll need one per tenant. This is a particularly useful strategy for those letting to younger people say the under 25s. It ties a responsible adult into the tenancy, making them accept some of the financial risks you're running when letting to youngsters.

WARNING ANECDOTE

At the lower end of the price spectrum it will often be necessary for landlords to let to younger, less experienced tenants occasionally and, for the under 25s you'll always *need* a parental guarantor.

Imagine my surprise when a late night call came through from a delightful couple. Purple scalding hot water was pouring through the ceiling and straight onto their bed! A hasty call to the plumber settled things down and I went to investigate. First, I placated the downstairs tenants. Next, I spoke to the plumber who'd switched off a young tenant's newly delivered washing machine at almost midnight and who was still laughing (though I couldn't join in I'm afraid). I confess, sometimes it takes even me a bit of time to see the funny side of things: and sometimes we're talking *years!*). Apparently, when asked by the plumber where he'd put the outlet pipe for the waste my new tenant had asked 'what outlet pipe?'

Finally, I visited my new youthful tenant in the upstairs bed-sitter. I calmly knocked on the door, which was opened by the proud owner of a bouncy new Rottweiler pup! Words were exchanged and the dog had to go.

I went home and called his mother, who'd signed the parental guarantor form. She wasn't happy. But then neither was I. In this business it sometimes pays dividends to be very firm. A few days later her cheque arrived and he soon moved home again.

People skills – you can't beat them in this business.

Break clauses

Although shorthold assured tenancies can be terminated after six months, some landlords (or tenants) want a break clause, say after three. This can be a precarious ground for landlords – is *not advised* and requires a specialist lease. Break clauses are a specialist facility, usually used by landlords and tenants letting and renting very expensive units of accommodation. No landlord should be beguiled into imagining that this is the thing they need to help them get round the very reasonable terms of the 1988 Housing Act and shorten the six month minimum fixed term. In truth, the overwhelming majority of independent landlords would do well to avoid getting themselves into areas of such unnecessary complexity (and units over £500 p.w. can't be assured shortholds anyway).

Whys and wherefores

Yet again, reading this lesson shouldn't take very long. Ordering your copy of the government's own guide book which verifies this information takes a matter of moments and, as the information is basic, it won't take long to read.

Beyond that, online sites give a huge amount of advice about being a landlord, but rarely cover actual leases – probably because when it comes down to it, there's really not much to say about such a simple document. If you would like to take a look at an off-the-peg variety, call Oyez (tel: 020 7556 3200) and order one. Postage takes around one day.

Further information

- Department for Communities and Local Government
  Officers in the Private Rented Housing Section at the Office of the Deputy Prime Minister can be extremely helpful if you telephone them on 0207 890 3000 and ask nicely. Call on their Free Literature number 0870 1226 236. Ask for a free catalogue – there are some other very useful free leaflets.

- Citizens Advice Bureau
  The Citizens Advice Bureau can also be helpful.

- The internet
  Online websites like *www.landlordzone.co.uk* and *www.rics.co.uk* or *www.rla.co.uk* are good places to research. Try also checking out the government's own website – it's surprisingly user friendly at *www.communities.gov.uk*. The issues around joint and several liability are often discussed on university websites under their accommodation advice sections – they can make very interesting reading. I find UCL or Bristol have good responsive sites.

How long did this take?

How long did it take to read this lesson and reassure yourself that an assured shorthold lease *guarantees* you possession at the end of the fixed term – 20 minutes? How long to consider what type of lease will suit you and where to obtain them – another 10? How long to familiarise yourself with a standard lease, when you've purchased one? Maybe half an hour – once only during a lifetime – they don't change much believe me. Anyone with the skills to read anything as complex as a daily newspaper can certainly understand a lease like these.

So, landlords can learn a great deal in just over an hour (remember, you're not aiming to sit a degree in landlord and tenant, just enough to run your tenancies effectively). Even the most anxious of first time landlords who may want to run through the process a couple of times should only need a few hours to get their heads around the details. I've never met a single landlord who failed at the lease hurdle. Everyone worries about it like mad the first time (and that's understandable) – then finds how easy it is and can't believe how they breezed through it when the time came. When you pause for a moment to consider how much an agency will charge you and your tenants for these processes it certainly isn't long.

— CHECKLIST/SUMMARY —

■ Ignore scaremongers. 1997 changed the legislation. Every new lease signed under the 1988 Housing Act is an assured *shorthold lease* – unless the tenant can prove to a court that you voluntarily gave them written proof that you offered them something with more rights.

■ Break clauses are unnecessary for investors. Avoid giving them.

■ Leases are important legal documents. Keep them safe.

■ Make sure your tenant understands their lease – this will help tenants to understand what's expected of them *during and at the end of their tenancy.*

■ Most leases are between one tenant and one landlord. Where agents are used, the lease may be between the agent and the tenant.

■ The advantages of an assured shorthold lease kick into place at the end of the initial 'fixed term'. Keeping this initial fixed term to six months offers the maximum *all round* benefits to landlords.

■ Always use a written lease and back it up with a Tenant Application Form (see Lesson 9), inventory and schedule of condition, giving both landlord and tenant a solid degree of protection from one another's idiosyncrasies.

- Don't kid yourself into believing you can set up a license operation, to avoid giving tenants any rights at all. It's surprisingly difficult.

- Don't photocopy off-the-peg leases, it's copyright theft and has been challenged. They're cheap and the more you buy the cheaper they become – but don't order too far in advance to save a few pounds because last year's lease may not be up to date. As a rule of thumb, buy new leases every six to nine months.

- Read and understand your lease. It isn't difficult – and if it is, change lease suppliers.

- Your paperwork can't override the basic framework of the 1988 Housing Act, whatever you try inserting as a clause.

- Give tenants enough time to read leases before expecting them to sign.

- Make sure you understand what the initial fixed term means and be wary of extending it beyond six months with new, unknown tenants.

- When leases do come to an end, either re-issue a new lease or allow the tenancy to become a statutory periodic one to retain the advantages of being beyond the fixed term.

- Make sure that leases are filled in correctly, signed in ink, dated and witnessed.

- Read Lesson 11 on grounds for possession – leases are not easy to get out of during that initial fixed term once they are signed.

- Make sure you have two leases per tenancy – one for the landlord, one for the tenant/s.

- If you let separately to more than one tenant you'll need a pair of leases for each tenancy.

- If you let out on joint and several liability – all sharers plus the landlord and witness(es) sign just two separate leases (one copy for the landlord, one copy for the tenants to keep).

- *Always* get legal documents witnessed.

■ By paying rent your tenant is buying a 'right to quiet enjoyment'. This needs to be respected by *all* landlords.

■ Always give tenants 24 hours' written notice of your intention to inspect or carry out repairs to their home.

■ Keep spare keys.

■ Even if you use an agent – keep spare keys.

■ Don't allow agents to bully you into offering an initial fixed term of more than six months. Assured shorthold leases do not necessarily need replacing at the end of the first six months. On the contrary, leaving the old lease in place often, if not always, gives landlords the most rapid access to obtaining possession should a problem suddenly arise.

■ If a year goes by under a statutory periodic tenancy and you feel a rent increase is necessary, get a form from Oyez for a rent increase and serve it on your tenant. Or download a form from *www.communities.gov.uk*. Tenants, however, may decide to move rather than paying more – and never forget – a bird in the hand...

Lesson 6

Advertising

Here's where we begin to get down to the nuts and bolts of being 'an independent'. Contact with customers needs to be made, once a property has been bought and set up. Rental valuations should have already been made as part of the purchase process (see Lesson 2: Mock advertising) and so – unless a significant time lag has arisen – it's time to get the ball rolling.

The *best rent* you'll get is one that's *sustainable* over a year. Set viable rent levels to maximise interest.

Don't overprice. Overpriced units stay empty and cost more than 100 per cent revenue every day. New landlords are often tempted to believe their unit's worth more than market rate. It's human nature to imagine that our precious unit is special. And a mistake. But pricing is not a precise science and needs careful reviewing because market conditions change all the time.

WARNING ANECDOTE

Having purchased two units in a new development, I advertised. A fantastic response meant that the first unit was let to the first viewer. Realising that I could have underestimated the rent I promptly got on the phone to the next few viewers, explaining that, due to the response, I would be asking for a 10 per cent increase in the advertised rent. Were they still interested? Indeed they were – and the second unit went that same evening. Rental valuations are a matter of local conditions and timing – in other words, the going rate locally. Easy to discover in an evening – and not some specialist trade secret.

However, I have *never* achieved that same higher rent level again – and I have tried – believe me. It was a glitch. So, be versatile. When demand's hot, you'll get premium rents – when things cool down, you won't. And being quick off the mark is yet another benefit of being independent.

First task

We need viewers and plenty of them because that gives us *choice* in who we let to. Advertising is the first point where differences between using agents and operating independently starts to work in the independent's favour. Our advertising can perfectly match each unit to appropriate tenants. And it's so simple it's hard to imagine the necessity of paying people a fortune to do it.

Second task – finding a venue to advertise in

Advertise in either the best local paper or the internet – or possibly both. A local set of abbreviations is likely to be in play, so read the adverts you've found and familiarise yourself with how things are done locally. Remember that there's a historic relationship between tenants and local newspaper advertising that the internet hasn't broken down yet, so don't rely exclusively on anything but print. The newspaper remains the main arena where tenants *always* look. In some areas you'll have to pay for advertising. In others, freebies have the widest readership. If you do have to pay, get a receipt or keep your credit/debit statement as these costs are tax deductible.

Effective advertising is the key to effective letting

Advertising is most effective when either extensive or accurately focused. Independent landlords must always concentrate on accuracy to avoid unnecessary costs. Leave the agents to pay for glossies and stick to the classifieds.

Effective advertising keeps voids to a minimum

Independent landlords need to keep their units filled because empty units lose real cash. Agents rely on volume, but you don't. Tenants can and do find *just* what they want in the classifieds and this is where to show them specifically what's on offer.

Tenants are consumers and as such, they're often discerning. This means you need to tell them what they need to know before someone else does. Landlords who aren't specific enough have their adverts ignored as tenants aren't certain what's on offer and – in a crowded market – they skip incomplete adverts. Which, for example, do you think would generate the best response?

Ford, 2 door, £1,000

or

Ford Escort. 4 years old. Low mileage. MOT. Taxed. £1,000

Applying the same principle to your property and that:

2-bedroom flat, Clapham

could be a dream home – or a nightmare. Could be in budget – or not. May be furnished – or empty. Tenants can't possibly know.

Detail matters

Don't waste weeks of lost rent to cut £10 off advertising costs. Conversely, going overboard is a waste of money. The knack is to avoid 'vague' while steering clear of 'wasteful'.

A word on advert wording

When using newspapers, work out your wording clearly and well in advance of making a call to the local paper to place it. *Never* advertise without including the costs. You'd be amazed how many people do so and it throws up two different problems.

1. The right tenant may not bother to call at all and move on down the column.
2. You'll get dozens of pointless calls and tie up the phone as many callers will be looking for something more . . . or less expensive.

Many newspapers use voicemail. You'll need to know exactly what you want to say to a machine and in what order or risk getting into a terrible muddle and forgetting some important detail, so write it out carefully beforehand. You might also want to try relocation agencies which don't always charge landlords. Or local employers like hospitals can be worth approaching direct. Safe properties can get themselves registered on accredited lists from local authorities, attracting tenants across the board.

What to say

Use local and *recognised* abbreviations, otherwise tenants won't understand what you mean. 'C/H' is centrally heated. 'S/C' is self-contained – an essential insertion for cheaper property, which often has shared facilities. 'Furn' for furnished, etc ('F/F' means down to the teaspoons and is a nightmare to control).

Clarity and succinctness are key. Always advertise the weekly rent for reasons explained earlier.

Take a look at the following examples.

Example 1.

---

2 bed-room flat, Clapham.
Furnished and centrally heated.
References/deposit required. Suit professionals.
Ring 0208 900 1000

Example 2.

---

2 bed-room S/C Furn. C/H period flat,
nr Clapham Common.
No children/pets/unemployed or under 25 yrs.
Refs. reqd. £275 pw. 4 wk. dep req. Suit 2
0208 900 1000

Example 1 indicates size and general area only. Too much unnecessary detail, which could have been abbreviated means this advert gives no clear idea of the kind of tenants required, yet simultaneously rejects 95 per cent of the population who aren't professionals. It gives no idea of the rent, nor any indication of the deposit.

Example 2 is much more to the point. Size matters in rentals. You've shown that the property is two bedroomed and near the common, rather than less expensive areas of Clapham. 'Furn' means basic furniture is provided. ('P/F' usually means that the basics, such as cooker, refrigerator carpets and curtains are included but this will need further clarification when potential tenants telephone. 'U/F' means unfurnished – but rental units will always require some white goods and should include carpets because no one will carpet your property on a six month lease.)

Example 2 explains that the unit is centrally heated (ie modern(ish). 'Suit 2' broadens the appeal beyond professionals. 'Over 25' removes the student sharers (unless you're happy to accept them).

Potential callers now have a much more specific idea of what's on offer, to whom and on what terms for broadly the same advertising cost. Explaining what you don't want cuts down the number of pointless calls. Adding the two words 'fire safety' and any other particularly useful issues like 'parking' and you get:

> **2 bedroom S/C Furn. C/H period flat,**
> **nr Clapham Common.**
> **S/C,F/F,C/H period flat**
> **(+fire safety+ off street parking)**
> **No children/pets/unemployed or under 25 yrs.**
> **Refs. reqd. £275 pw. 4 wk. dep req. Suit 2**
> **No agents please**
> **0208 900 1000**

This separates your unit in three short syllables from the numerous rogue landlords out there (provided of course that you've spent the £30-£40 and installed smoke alarms, extinguisher and fire blanket, which you should – to protect both your tenants and your investment). Don't abbreviate details of fire safety, it's good copy, though most tenants won't pay extra for the privilege of somewhere safe. In large cities always include parking if it's available, as this is a considerable selling point for car conscious tenants.

And, unless you want to attract them, always add 'No agents' or half your calls will be from them – and it's *tenants* you're after.

Now, tailor this to suit *your* unit and place your advertisement.

Be available on the first day the advertisement appears

Answerphones are no substitute for a landlord's voice, and your children or the broken English of the au pair will often make tenants move onto the next advert.

Some landlords only provide mobile phone numbers. However, some tenants are extremely wary of the 'mobile' landlord – that entity who disappears the moment the boiler breaks down. If you want to use a mobile always combine it with a landline, so that tenants feel that you have a base somewhere and will be contactable in the future. I cannot emphasise strongly enough how important it is to give out the right 'vibes' to tenants at this initial stage. With virtually no security of tenure, high rents and a notoriously unregulated industry, tenants can bolt like startled deer if they get the slightest sense of even more potential problems ahead. A landlord you can't track down is the last thing someone paying out a thousand pounds a month wants.

Good psychology in tenant dealings is vital

All this may sound daft to that confident young businessman building up a portfolio of property but believe me, these aspects of management psychology matter. Trust is a rare commodity in our industry – the more of it you can make your tenants feel, the less likely you are to have problems.

Tenants can move on very quickly for something they want. With a list of a dozen potentials, they'll often keep calling numbers till they hear a voice they can ask for details. They call from work during the day and often call well into the evening when they get home. They rarely leave call back numbers. If you're not willing to take calls past 8 pm, take the phone off the hook rather than become irritable. People will often call back on an engaged tone – it's a sign that other people are also interested – a positive vibe.

But what do I say to them, when they call?

Be polite, informative and businesslike – a few pleasantries can oil the wheels of any deal. Ask what they want to know about the property. Explain a few details and then, if they're still interested, ask a few questions yourself. Novices should have a pen and paper by the phone with a list of questions. Scribble the caller's name on it and start asking. Ticks for positive answers, crosses for negative replies. If the call produces more negative than positive responses, don't arrange a viewing.

This first phone call can, for an experienced landlord, be as far as it goes.

Here are a few question suggestions.

- Where do people work?
- How long have they worked there?
- Where do they live now?
- Whether or not they've rented before. (Simply because rental virgins can sometimes make quite challenging tenants, so you need to talk them through the process very thoroughly if you take them.)
- When do they need accommodation from.
- If you're willing to accept young people, explain you'll want a guarantor for owed rent, damage and outstanding bills.
- Ask whom they'll be using.
- Always ask if callers have referees and if they will have any objections to a paying for a credit check.
- The above also applies to a Tenant Application Form.
- Make sure to ask if they have the funds for a deposit and the advance rent – a surprising number don't, so check before you waste time on a viewing.
- Explain that, if they like the unit, you won't be able to hold it for them without a week's rent on account. This is called a holding deposit.
- Get a phone number for security and so you can contact them if you've already let the unit to save unnecessary viewings.

Don't make appointments with people you don't like the sound of, or who are unwilling to talk to you. These are not intrusive questions, they're an essential part of the deal and you don't need a taciturn tenant.

If you get a chance, explain that you're not an agent and that you won't be making them pay out for a long list of additional charges, but simply taking reasonable precautionary steps on issues like credit checks and bank references which have low genuine costs.

Reasonable people understand reasonable behaviour and the one thing you're trying to find in a tenant is *reasonableness*.

Find out how quickly a tenant wants to move in

Know exactly when callers want to move. Some tenants have no real intention of moving unless they find something better than they have so would need weeks to serve notice on their old place.

Others will need something this week, or will be moving into the area that weekend, or are currently living in a B&B. It's an important issue to tease out. Don't go rushing out for people who can't move in for weeks: show them the unit when you're already making a trip, say just before or just after a serious viewing.

A tip to avoid time-wasters

For some unknown reason, around a third of people who make appointments simply don't turn up. Try insisting that viewers telephone you *one hour* before their appointment to confirm they're still coming. And make it clear that without that confirmation, you won't be driving over. That does help cut out the time-wasters.

For landlords re-advertising on an existing tenant's notice

This entire process should be started as soon as your tenant advises you they'll be leaving. That way you should have someone signed up well before you have an empty unit on your hands – and this gives those tenants who'll need to give notice in their existing unit a genuine shot – thereby increasing your potential customers.

Notifying existing tenants about viewings

Give your existing tenant a letter outlining dates and times that you'll be entering for viewings. Make it something reasonable like Thursday and Friday evenings, between 6 pm and 8 pm. This gives fair notice and isn't too disruptive – don't forget, your existing tenant still lives here and pays rent. So make short windows that suit your own timescale then advise your tenants.

Note: Don't hold property for someone who claims to be interested but won't sign a Tenant Application Form or hand over a holding deposit. Tenants can *say* anything – it's what they *do* that matters.

Independents take their background checks seriously. That's why we don't do 30 viewings like ARLA claims to be doing. Don't waste time and petrol driving back and forth to open doors for people you're going to reject anyway – ask first. Demand for units can be incredibly variable. Sometimes the phone will ring off the hook. Others, you'll be doing well to take a call a day. If your rent level is right, you should be able to generate a minimum of five or six interested callers per advert.

Holding deposits

These are a simple concept. If you decide that you like a tenant and they like your property, don't take it off the market without having some financial cover. Without an interim payment you shouldn't turn down a single other tenant or viewing – let alone stop advertising. This is a holding deposit and it needs to be sufficiently big to cover your costs if the tenant changes their mind. A minimum of one week's rent is advised. There are three things you then need to remember.

1. Always give the tenant a receipt for their holding deposit that states that this fee is non returnable if the *tenant* changes their mind or if references and/or credit checks are unsatisfactory.

2. That it *is* refundable if *the landlord* changes their mind for no good reason.

3. That your new tenant understands that this holding deposit will be deducted from the full deposit when the transaction is complete, leases signed and monies exchanged. In other words, if a tenant provides a £250 holding deposit on a unit with a £1,000 damages

deposit, the deposit balance due will thus be £750 when the deal is finally done.

Once money has changed hands you can be reasonably certain that the tenant has made a financial commitment to the property. Some landlords continue viewings to establish the fallback position of a second very interested potential tenant. However, it is highly unreasonable and may in some circumstances even be illegal to take holding deposits from more than one party at a time. Be up-front, and when you've given your word – always keep it. You may be scrutinising tenants – but trust me, they're returning the compliment and trust matters a great deal with assets this size held on a few weeks' rent.

Mutual respect makes tenancies run more smoothly

Again and again I stress that a position of mutual respect works best. Nervous tenants can quickly become irritable – even hostile and that's the worst position for a landlord to find themselves in. Don't trade short-term profits for long-term reputations. It's commercial suicide.

Think safety first

Ask everyone who has made an appointment for a contact phone number and try to insist on a landline somewhere. It may sound a little neurotic but, as a female landlord often conducting viewings in empty buildings, I do prefer to spend the couple of minutes it takes to suggest calling them back at work or maybe confirming our arrangements later on in the evening on a landline wherever possible (for a few more safety tips, see Lesson 8: Viewings).

Once I've asked these questions, what next?

The next step is to agree appointments. Many tenants prefer to see units in the early evening or at weekends. This can be a significant advantage for independents as we're open when agents are often closed. Make your appointments for as soon as is practicable for both parties – tenants can get fixed up quite quickly so don't miss the boat. If you're lucky enough to get several appointments on the same day – make them half an hour apart.

Supply side gluts

For the first time anyone in the business can recall, some areas are experiencing genuine supply side gluts. If you're unlucky enough to be in this situation, the only advice that makes sense is to adjust (drop) rent levels. However, you may still experience difficulty at a lower rent – especially in that interim period where you're having to re-advertise time and time again to establish a viable rent. In these circumstances, experienced landlords change the format of their advertising at least every two weeks to avoid the unit becoming stale. The *last* advertisement you need is the same one week after week that tenants see hanging about. So, change the wording slightly in some way. Let's take a look at our original unit:

---

2 bedroom S/C Furn C/H period flat, (+ fire safety) nr Clapham Common.
No children/pets/unemployed or under 25 yrs.
Refs. reqd. £275 pw. 4 wk. dep req. Suit 2.
No agents Please
0208 900 1000

After a couple of weeks, try making changes without losing the essence of the information – for example:

Victorian apartment, nr Clapham Common.
Well presented Furn & C/H & smoke alarms.
£275 per week. Over 25s only with deposit
(4 wks) and refs.
Sorry – no unemployed, pets, children, agents.
08473 624 952 or 0208 900 1000

The same basic information, plus a few changes and most people won't notice the repeat.

And *never* tell anyone who calls that the unit is taken until you have at the very least a holding deposit and some references that stack up. If you *think* you've found the right person, you can always explain and ask additional callers for their number and say you'll call back if the deal doesn't go through.

Whys and wherefores

This lesson is one of the easiest. It shouldn't take you more than a few minutes reading time. I'm sorry to say but I know of no other guide that goes into this much detail for you to double-check this information. You will, however, need to spend some time and energy getting hold of appropriate papers to help you to frame your advertisement. Drawing up an advertisement itself is easy. Include what tenants need to know and exclude what you don't want.

— CHECKLIST/SUMMARY —

■ Always use the most suitable venue for your advertising. Don't cut costs and end up with no interested parties.

■ Landlords who have just been served notice of their existing tenant's intention to leave should begin advertising immediately.

■ Make sure your advertisement contains enough detail to filter out callers who won't interest you. Always double-check important details (say employment status) on the phone.

■ Be specific about what the unit offers, moving in costs and security checks.

■ Always include the *weekly* rental costs – (it's broadly the same psychology as offering something for £1.99 – rather than £2).

■ Write out your advertisement clearly in case you're speaking to the newspaper's automated service and keep a copy by the phone.

■ Request receipts from advertisers – they're tax deductible.

- If repeat advertising becomes necessary, change the format of your advertising.

- Try to be available, especially when the advertisement is new.

- Try to give a landline – tenants don't like mobiles much.

- Be friendly but businesslike. Make a list of, then ask the questions you *need* to and establish the ground rules for the checks you'll be making before arranging a pointless viewing. You'll need a separate sheet for each caller which we'll use later.

- Try not to overwhelm tenants on the phone; it's not a personality contest to be won by landlords.

- Make appointments for as soon as possible...like today/tomorrow to avoid tenants finding something else in the meantime.

- Independent landlords can make evening appointments which can be a distinct advantage in a tight or fast-moving market – use your advantages.

Lesson 7

Inventories, Schedules of Condition and Property Profiles

Taking stock

Like any business, there comes a time to stocktake. If you're using a computer, so much the better. These make the business of inventory production a piece of cake. If you don't have these documents on a PC do make sure that, having typed everything out once, you don't give all the copies out to tenants, or you'll have nothing to photocopy for the next let.

It is time to begin yet another of the numerous small tasks that are part and parcel of being a flourishing private landlord. Don't feel daunted. This is extremely simple stuff – once you've learned how to do it, you'll wonder why you ever paid anyone else. These tasks constitute the nitty-gritty that help to keep your property well cared for – your tenants safe and your own finances protected.

What paperwork are you suggesting landlords use to complement their leases?

I (and everyone sensible) use three simple but different documents. It's a belt and braces approach, which should not only protect your property and its contents – but also help cut down management time with new tenants learning the unit's idiosyncrasies.

The first of these protections – *the inventory* – is best known and understood. Most agents don't even bother with the second as a separate document – a *Schedule of Condition* – despite the fabric of the building being far more valuable than most of the contents will ever be. And most won't even have heard of the third, a *Property Profile*. However, that's a problem for agency clients, not my readers. Here, you're strongly advised to use all three components. Additionally, using all three makes you look competent and that's important psychology too. Tenants don't want to deal with amateurs.

An accurate record of the unit's condition at the start of new tenancies helps landlords and tenants negotiate what can sometimes be tricky waters at the end of the tenancy. It's your protection and the tenant's protection in black and white – and it *matters!*

How digital images help both parties

These days, I always take digital pictures of units prior to tenants signing leases and ask tenants to initial and date them as they move in. That way there's little room for debate about how things were when they accepted the unit. And again, if this sounds like a 'faff', remember that you're handing over a property here, not a second-hand bike and it's got to be worth those ten extra minutes.

Using your documents as a carrot and stick

Landlords need to learn to use these documents. An inventory isn't only a way to prevent damage – it's an opportunity for a tenant to get their deposit back. Far too many landlords don't appreciate the level of sheer antipathy that's developing out there in our marketplace as tenants learn over and over that their hard-earned deposit will evaporate however well they behave. This is bad property management; encouraged by amateurs and crooks. What's more, their behaviour is creating a dreadful climate, where tenants feel justified in refusing to pay the final few weeks rent on the assumption they'll never see their deposit again anyway. Which actually means that the process of taking deposits becomes utterly useless.

Good landlords do good business because they behave in a reasonable manner. Strangely, they often get the pick of the tenants as word spreads. So, compile your Inventory. Draw up your Schedule of Condition. Put together a Property Profile then use them *from the first day you accept a tenant* as a means of explaining exactly how you want the property returned in order to facilitate a full deposit return. It won't work every time – but it does work *most* of the time.

The inventory

This can be drawn up by the landlord (or agent, for a fee) or, by a wholly independent third party Inventory Service. This is an excellent idea for expensive units, however, it is pricey. Landlords wanting to consider this should find a service (usually the *Yellow Pages*) and discuss terms. Landlords often share these costs on a 50–50 basis with tenants, as a binding inventory is a *shared benefit*.

The independent inventory service

Independent inventories are by no means necessary on most units; they can, however, prevent the awful arguments in complex, pricey units with high specification finishes. Each party agrees to be bound by decisions taken by the independent compiler right from the start. Independent inventory clerks will draw up a comprehensive inventory before tenants move in – agreed by both landlord and tenant as accurate – then revisit when the property is empty at the end of the tenancy and examine the property and contents for damage, then estimate realistic costs of restitution (if any). It's a worthwhile option for landlords to consider for units with costly finishes which are unlikely to be covered by a tenant's (even six weeks') deposit. Floor finishes are particularly prone to steel stiletto heels and black granite worktops don't look so dandy when no one used a chopping board. Restitution on both cost a fortune. When items like these are in place, I'd always use an independent service.

Inventories for the vast majority of rentals

In most cases, a straightforward landlord-typed inventory works perfectly well given that tenants don't *have* to sign anything they don't agree with. It needs to be clear, concise, easy to understand and accurate.

A personal preference is for a few strategic snaps on a digital camera taken on moving in day with the landlord's and tenant's signatures and the date on the back (you may even have these witnessed too) and retained by the landlord in case of dispute. These can prove very useful in the parental guarantor scenario, where the defensive parent turns up full of rage that little Suzie's deposit has gone walkabouts.

Most of the time in this business, you'll be challenged. Again – don't take it personally. Usually all it takes to diffuse an awkward situation is something tangible to prove that your conduct was reasonable (which will always be the last thing anyone's expecting). Likewise, taking photographs of *all* damage when it does arise can be very useful especially when placed alongside the previous photographs you took before the tenant took possession. Most people when confronted with something irrefutable will accept fair costs and so will any new deposit system.

How to manage an inventory process

Landlords need to walk their newly accepted tenants through the inventory, allowing comment by the tenant to be inserted – if for example, you've forgotten to note a problem or missed something. This is a shared value document.

Both landlord and tenant need to be happy with its accuracy when the inventory comes to be signed. Make certain the unit is very clean – stale smelling units give a sloppy impression and encourage poor standards in return.

Provide everything sensible but tenants should bring their own linen, cooking utensils, towels and small items like kettles and toasters – mainly because it's too tricky to keep to a high standard (and will often go walkies). Secondly, because tenants prefer to be able to customise units into homes. Thirdly, because most tenants don't want to use someone else's toaster or bedding. And fourthly, because everything electrical for example that you supply as a landlord comes with a safety liability (see Lesson 12: The *serious* responsibilities).

Set your units up *realistically* before letting them out.

Always include essentials like bathroom and bedroom mirrors – because not doing so will give the tenant few alternatives but to try to fix something up themselves and *all tenants should be actively discouraged from DIY.*

Protect your interests by providing *a reasonably equipped unit* that a tenant can move into and live in realistically, simply because most deposits won't be anything like sufficient to cover the re-plastering of walls – and large bills are inevitably disputed.

How to compile an inventory

1. Start the inventory with the full address of the unit:

**Inventory of contents
for Flat 6, 47 Howard Road, Teddington, MX2 4HP**

2. Add the following rider about cleanliness at the beginning:

All contents are clean, undamaged and in good condition (except where otherwise noted on this inventory). Internal windows clean on acceptance.

3. Then list – room by room, the entire contents and the condition of them as follows, reinforcing at every opportunity the initial cleanliness and presentation, as in the couple of room by room examples given here:

Bedroom
Sleepeze double bed – good condition, mattress clean
Mattress cover, freshly laundered (please wash and refit before vacating)
Carpet, blue cord, in perfect condition (except one small cigarette burn to LHS of bedside cabinet)
Curtains, grey blue – pair of (clean)
Curtain track and gliders
Blind – matching above curtains. Working mechanics
2 bedside cabinets – grey/blue – a small coffee ring to rear RH corner of LHS cabinet
Light fitting – working with three working bulbs.
2 double fitted wardrobes, unmarked and in excellent condition
2 coat racks, complete and packed (if required) in fitted wardrobe (please re-pack and return to boxes on vacation of premises)
1 small dressing table (no marks)
1 full length mirror, fixed to wall
2 picture hooks (please don't fit more)
1 smoke alarm (battery working)

Kitchen

All fitted units and cupboards clean

Cooker – clean on acceptance

Refrigerator – cleaned and defrosted on acceptance

Microwave – clean

1 pair small chequered curtains plus curtain pole and rings (clean)

1 small net curtain (please wash and re-hang on vacation)

Vinyl floor covering (in good condition)

Service Automatic washing machine/dryer (service contract details in top drawer)

C/H boiler (Landlord's Gas Safety Certificate (tenant copy) plus service contract details in top drawer)

Fitted chrome towel rail

Light fittings (three halogen bulbs fitted and working)

1 smoke detector (batteries working)

1 carbon monoxide detector (batteries working)

1 domestic sized fire extinguisher and fire blanket

Go through each room in a similar manner

Make issues like defrosting refrigerators and cleaning out ovens thoroughly clear from the outset. They *take hours* for the landlord's cleaner to do – and tenants always baulk at the true cost of cleaning.

Continue in this way, itemising everything as you go and making small comments about condition. Encourage incoming tenants to check through the inventory to avoid misunderstandings later. The order of the rooms is irrelevant but remember – anything not on the inventory is *not* safeguarded by the document.

When the inventory is complete, add the following, which ought to safeguard you for fire insurance purposes:

ABSOLUTELY NO FREE STANDING FIRES OR HEATERS OF <u>ANY</u> TYPE TO BE BROUGHT INTO THE BUILDING UNDER ANY CIRCUMSTANCES. They invalidate the Fire Insurance and may constitute Grounds for Possession.

Using the inventory as a reminder board

If you've any other reminders you wish to make, this is a good place to insert them. For example, where flats are concerned, it's usually a good idea to mention that tenants bringing in TVs and stereos should use them in a manner that won't disturb other residents. You may have a car park agreement you wish to insert here. 'No decorating without the landlord's written consent' is useful. 'No furniture to be removed without the landlord's written consent' is another you should consider. 'Unauthorised repairs will *not* be reimbursed — please contact landlord first'. Most landlords can think of a few bits and pieces to add here.

Finally add something along the lines of:

> *This statement of condition of the contents (otherwise known as the inventory) is an accurate account of the condition of all items offered for use as part of the furnished tenancy at . . . . [insert property address] and agreed by both landlord and tenant as accurate on . . . . [insert date here] and witnessed by [witness signature and date] . . . .*

> *Tenants are reminded of the requirement to return the contents in the same condition (wear and tear excepted), when they vacate the premises. Please replace light bulbs if required and clean interior windows. All tenants leaving the property and contents in an equivalent condition to today's date will receive a full deposit return to an accurate forwarding address in cheque form. Tenants will be responsible for all damage and cleaning required to return the property to the condition of the day of acceptance of these terms.*

> *Signed [tenant] . . . .   Signed [landlord] . . . .*

> *Date . . . .*

> *Witnessed by . . . .   [date)] . . . .*

(Wherever possible use someone you, as landlord, know as a witness. Using the tenant's friend can understandably lead to problems where disputes arise.)

Two final notes.

1. As with all legally binding documents, where the inventory can run to several pages add page 1 of 4, page 2 of 4, page 3 of 4 to the bottom right-hand side of each page. Both the tenant and you should initial each page.

2. These documents will probably need to form part of the information about which organisation will be safeguarding your tenant's deposits soon. Keep an eye on the legislation via *www.communities.gov.uk* and make sure that the appropriate information is given to tenants at the same time as their inventories and leases (as soon as the government releases that 'appropriate' wording) see Lesson 10: Deposits).

Schedules of Condition

Next we have a shorter – though sometimes more valuable document which landlords should try to keep to one or two pages. It's a document that will be of immense value should tenants damage the decorative features or the actual fabric of the building – a much more valuable beast than a sofa.

Here's where being an independent gives you back genuine control. Make a detailed list of the building's decorative standard and fixtures here, rather than the contents and keep the two documents separate. As with the inventory, here are a few ideas for you to keep in mind when formulating your own schedule. Head it up with your property's address and off you go. (Remember the page numbering rule.)

Honesty's the best policy

Make everything crystal clear from the outset. It's always better to get these matters ironed out before a tenancy begins rather than mid-way through acrimonious deposit negotiations.

When tenants leave

Simply reverse the entire process after your tenants have vacated.

Schedule of Condition
of the property known as: Flat 6, 47 Howard Road, Teddington, MX2 4HP
and dated on the first day of the
tenancy between the parties herewith as accurate.

Lounge

Walls, plain cream, plastered and emulsioned finish. Unmarked (except for small areas of damage behind sofa head. Three picture hooks provided. Please fix *nothing* extra to the walls (including pins and blutac), as they damage the decorative finish.

Stripped floorboards in good condition (with the exception of a small area of wear damage between bay window and hallway).

One casement window – in working order with working catches and window locks (key on LHS window cill of bay).

Paintwork white gloss – several small chips to doorframe – otherwise in good condition throughout.

Ceiling – white emulsion – unmarked. (This may be an odd one to include but it's amazing how many beer/coke stains hit the ceiling.)

Bathroom

White suite comprising bath, toilet, low-level cistern and basin plus chrome taps and showerhead. All in excellent condition on acceptance. (Please do *not* use abrasives on any appliances/fittings.)

Vinyl flooring – in perfect condition.

Bedroom

Walls plain cream, plastered and emulsioned finish. Three shelves fitted into recess. No damage but crack between window frame and skirting board is noted.

Fitted wardrobes – wood veneer (condition as indicated on inventory).

Sash window – both top and bottom sections in full working order. Please open carefully. Sash lock fitted and working on acceptance.

Paintwork – white gloss – unmarked.

Ceiling – white emulsion – no marks.

Fitted full length mirror.

(Etc. Don't forget to include hallways – burglar alarms – and anything of value not mentioned in the inventory.)

Date...................................

Name of tenant ....

Name of landlord ....   Witnessed by......................

Date...................................

Note: *Always conclude this Schedule of Condition document with the following statement: Nothing whatsoever to be fixed to the walls. No shelves, picture hooks, drawing pins or blutac as these may spoil the decorative finish and render the tenant liable for substantial repair costs.*

Example of a Schedule of Condition.

Don't carry out end of tenancy audits until the tenants have vacated entirely and handed back the keys. You can't do it effectively when the tenant is breathing down your neck – or between cardboard boxes. Check your copies, noting any discrepancies between when tenants moved in and when they moved out. That discrepancy (which must be some way beyond normal wear and tear) constitutes what you can legitimately make reasonable charges for. From April 2007, the tenancy deposit scheme will make these decisions on our behalf in cases of dispute – see Lesson 10: Deposits.

Property Profile

And finally we have a document aimed entirely at making our new tenants feel welcome plus, and rather more importantly, saving a myriad of phone calls when tenants first move in. Pro-active management saves time and numerous phone calls.

The Property Profile's purpose is self-explanatory and needs no signatures. It's a simple, effective way to help tenants settle in rather than a legal document.

This is where to incorporate all those little quirks that could generate a concerned phone call. The dimmer switch that's perfectly safe but no longer dims. The loo handle you need to hold down for two or three seconds to make a perfectly good toilet flush. Not many of us manage to get everything absolutely spot on in our own homes, let alone chase up every single idiosyncrasy in, say, a three-bedroomed Victorian terrace we're renting out for our pensions.

Here's a perfect example. This Property Profile was compiled by a very conscientious landlord who successfully ran a single tenancy throughout a two-year volunteer programme in Albania. Something like this will be appreciated by your tenants and save you hassle. A good place to leave them is on a dining room table – in plain sight for moving in day.

Property profile
[Address]

Loft

1. Houses cold and hot water storage. Note: it is a small tank and holds three quarters of a bath full of hot water.
2. The light switch is clearly visible and on the left-hand side, just by the access hole. I'd prefer you not to store items here.

Landing

1. The switch for immersion heater is by front bedroom.
2. If there's any very heavy rain, a few drops can squeeze round the skylight – not enough to worry about.
3. Central heating thermostat on LHS of back bedroom door.

Front bedroom

1. The bed is new. Please wash the cover before vacating.
2. There are drawers under the bed. Inside is an electric fan for the summer and an iron.

Back bedroom

1. Cupboard houses central heating boiler, with controls. Instruction leaflet on left-hand side shelf. Due to its quaint location, in very strong winds the pilot light can sometimes get blown out! Instructions for re-lighting on page 7 of the manual.
2. The boiler is covered by a service contract with British Gas. Call them out if you have any problems at all with the heating or hot water. The service contract details are stored in the kitchen drawers along with Landlord's Gas Safety Certificate on this and other gas appliances.
3. This spare bed isn't new and left-hand leg is a bit wonky so, if you have a problem, try a novel under that leg.

Bathroom

1. Toilet fills slowly (about five minutes) so don't expect to flush in quick succession.
2. Thermostat on shower can be a bit awkward – but it definitely won't scald you.
3. Radiator sometimes needs bleeding in here. Bleed key on window cill.

(page 1 of 2)

Example of a Property Profile.

Living room front
1. Electricity meter in small cupboard.
2. Chimney very effective. If the winter evenings get to you, slide up the chimney cover (stick your hand up and push gently). There's wood and a bit of coal in the cellar. Help yourself.

Living room rear
1. Gas coal fire very convincing. *Don't throw anything on it*!

Kitchen
1. Top drawer has service contracts and instructions for everything (washer/dryer, dishwasher etc).
2. Middle drawer has list of emergency tradesmen. Please don't call anyone out without contacting Lesley Henderson, on 01635 878 760 who'll authorise – otherwise, as I'm volunteering for two years and not exactly flush, you'll be responsible for unauthorised costs.

(Author's note: useful for landlords setting up distance management–otherwise delete entirely.)

Cellar
Gas meter here. Plus fire goods.

Backyard
Dustbin men come *Mondays*. You need to put black bags onto front path or they won't collect.

Alf lives next door. He's nice. He has a spare key.

There's a table and chairs in the cellar for al fresco dining (if it ever stops raining).

For emergencies contact Lesley Henderson on 01635 878 760

For absolute disasters if Lesley's not around call Celia Rowsham on 01635 824 964 or Mick O'Leary on 01849 674 544.

Note: don't give these phone numbers to anyone else.
Hope you enjoy living here as much as I do.

Signed. . . . .

(page 2 of 2)

Example of a Property Profile (continued).

And that's a welcome and a half! Her informal yet helpful style encouraged her tenants to enjoy their home, whilst simultaneously pointing up their own liabilities. Two young tenants lived there happily, paid their rent each month and, on hearing Samantha would be returning via a letter of notice, moved out leaving the place just as they'd found it. What's called a win–win arrangement. What's more, her outgoing tenants bought her half a ton of coal and a stack of logs as a thank you. In return, they received a full deposit refund and an invaluable glowing reference from their former landlord.

Customer care is cost effective

Landlords sell the single most expensive commodity in the market-place, yet many spend hardly any time on customer care – while Tesco goes to some lengths to sell you a tube of Smarties. Give it a shot – I find it *usually* pays dividends.

Whys and wherefores

This lesson is filled with perfectly straightforward tools, none of which takes long. In total, it shouldn't have taken more than 15 minutes to read. However, compiling inventories, Schedules and a Property Profile can take a while the first time you make one.

Every landlord needs to have *a good written picture* of their properties. Deposit returns are one of the most contentious areas for landlords, tenants and agents. Even when using agencies, ensure that you have agreed their inventory *yourself*, and have a copy of it prior to any letting.

— CHECKLIST/SUMMARY —

- Always compile your own inventory or get a copy of the agent's and agree it. It's the only record that counts at the conclusion of tenancies.

- If your property is a high-end unit, most large cities have companies who offer an independent inventory service.

- Take tenants through the inventory – between both of you, you shouldn't miss much.

■ Draw up (or insist that your agent does) a Schedule of Condition, content inventories alone are incomplete.

■ Make sure both parties have a copy of each document and that both are signed, witnessed and dated to make them legally binding.

■ Anything you've contracted to provide, for example a washing machine or fridge needs to be kept in working order by you, unless tenants have broken them by abuse.

■ Service contracts can be cheaper and more convenient for everyone. Providing the tenant with service contracts means that you won't get bothered so much.

■ Damage of any kind is chargeable to the tenant. For example, a failed washing machine pump is a landlord liability – that same pump blocked by the tenant (say, by hairpins) makes this the *tenant's* liability.

■ Try to design a Property Profile to help your tenants settle in. It will help avoid a stream of trivial phone calls and it's a nice welcoming style.

■ Remember – everything mentioned on the inventory is provided by the landlord and should be insured by them.

■ Read the whole of this lesson – it's in your interests to protect your own possessions.

Lesson 8

Viewings

After your advertising

You should have a short list of tenants who want to take a look at your unit, appointments plus names and contact telephone numbers for each party on your questions lists, which you should take along with you to viewings as a reminder. Keep all contact numbers safe. They can often save re-advertising if your chosen tenant is unable to provide good references or backs out.

The benefits of flexibility

Independent landlords offer huge benefits for tenants as their viewing times aren't confined to office hours. Many tenants find evenings and weekends much more convenient, particularly if they have a job – and most of us want employed tenants. Therefore, make the most of your advantages. Arrange viewings to suit your tenants (within reason). Often these will be in the evening and a few tricks of the trade can help present properties to their best advantage.

Presentation for viewings

We've seen enough recently about property presentation to bore us all to death. However, as I write this guide, I'm making a few assumptions.

1. That anyone conscientious enough to buy a guide isn't letting out a dirty dump.

2. Rental units should almost always be furnished. They should also have reasonable, legally safe furniture (see Lesson 12: The *serious* responsibilities).

3. They won't be over-equipped. Beds, sofas, carpets, curtains, storage – maybe extra kitchen equipment, dishwashers, washing machines – whatever is cost effective and will earn its money in rent.

4. Don't buy anything expensive, such as kitchen cupboards, drapes or carpets – unless in *very* high specification units. Ikea or an ex-catalogue shop, even decent second-hand that complies with the furnishing regulations, are fine.

5. Buy decent but not expensive beds and provide a freshly washed cotton mattress cover (tenants won't sleep on a rubber cover – they'll heave it off and stuff it under the bed).

Cleanliness matters

I'm also assuming that landlords have enough sense to make sure that all rental units are spotlessly clean. Besides the obvious drawbacks of competition, tenants have a basic right to, and fully expect clean and tidy as standard. *Anything less and your unit's value per week will plummet – along with the calibre of tenants willing to move in.*

On sunny days, open curtains and pop a vanilla pod in the oven for ten minutes to make the place smell lived in. Check for dust – a sure giveaway in vacant units – even a wipe with your sleeve can make a unit look sparkly again. Don't expect tenants to leave places clean if they weren't clean when they moved in.

On chilly evenings, draw the curtains, *make sure the heating is switched on* and turn on a couple of lamps to make the place feel like someone's home. No tenant is going to appreciate shivering their way through a ten-minute viewing to save you fifty pence on the gas bill.

Possession isn't all it's cracked up to be

Rental property needs occupants to earn its keep. Having empty property is like buying a cab then keeping it in the garage. So, put yourself out a bit. A great deal of money depends on a tenant's first impression. Your unit certainly doesn't have to be extravagant or expensive to make it worth renting, but comfortable feeling units always find new tenants fastest.

If your existing tenant is still living there

For those of you conducting viewings whilst a tenant is in place, make sure you've given your outgoing tenant plenty of notice of viewing appointments. If you've had a good relationship, you might even ask them to wash up. Otherwise, a few words about untidiness and a helpless smile before you enter a clothes dump with a kitchen covered with yesterday's washing up will often work. Assure viewers that the unit will be scrubbed prior to their check in and they'll usually have the good sense to look past clutter (or show them your photos). If necessary and you're getting a good 'feel' about a tenant who has turned up with a landlord reference and some cash for a holding deposit for example, the offer of new carpet in the living room can often work a treat. Cord is so cheap, it's virtually disposable – and looks brilliant if laid properly.

WARNING ANECDOTE

During one of my recent courses an experienced landlord of some years scoffed audibly at the suggestion that it was remotely possible to let units while tenants were still in place. His units – he assured us all – were complete dumps during tenancies.

It's hard to reconcile the mindset of an involved landlord who collects rent, who is around property occasionally and is on reasonably good terms with tenants with that of someone who lets out a building, then never goes near the place unless there's a disaster. Buildings should *not* be absolute dumps when tenants live there. This landlord was a perfect example of what shouldn't be happening. Every landlord/agent should be making quarterly inspections of units. If things are getting a little squalid, mention how difficult they're going to find it to pull the unit into shape before leaving and start calculating how large a hole this might make in their deposit. I *guarantee* either comment will get the vacuum cleaner out.

Let's get back to those viewings

For those of us with a list of two or three appointments, it's usually best to switch on the lights/heating then return to wait in the car. Novice landlords, who didn't quite get through their list of questions when this tenant first called would do well to refresh their memories from their notes. A viewing is the first meeting point in what can become a long business relationship. The last thing you need to appear to be is a novice. Tenants feel more comfortable with landlords who know what they're doing.

Trusting your gut when meeting tenants

The car also makes an excellent vantage point from which to take an unnoticed peek at your new tenant, *before they see you*. From this moment onward it's down to instinct and you must learn to trust it. If someone makes you feel remotely uncomfortable in any way, pass. I repeat – pass. Even if it's your *only* viewing that week. Instinct isn't just about prejudices, sometimes it's your synapses making faster mental connections than you can rationally keep up with and churning out warnings. You're a landlord not a psychologist and you don't want to have to endure an adrenaline rush every time you need to make a necessary visit.

If a smart looking couple arrive in a hatchback with a pet security screen, you can bet they won't be mentioning the bulldog they've just dropped off at their mother's. You get my drift?

It's *amazing* what an impression you can get of people in these first few, unmonitored seconds. Unconsciously, we monitor people all the time, make judgements, decide who we feel comfortable with and who gives us the heebie-jeebies. Gut instinct can be your most valuable tool in this trade.

Put bluntly, you're looking for someone you'd be comfortable dealing with every four weeks for six months. Many a decision to say 'no' is based on these first impressions or of seeing something that gets your hackles up or that troubles you in some indefinable way.

You're looking for tenants who are a reasonable match with your requirements, your unit and to some extent, your character – but *not* for a friend. Many landlords happily take kids/bulldogs and budgerigars. But leave your *prejudices* to your choice of daily paper – very bad for business.

And then? After that initial sneaky inspection, the rest is simple. Open the door.

Advice for the ladies

Step back and let men in first – leave the front door open – I always have a doorstop in my bag to kick in place to hold entrance doors open. If that sounds too premeditated, pull the doormat up so the door can't slam shut. Never let a stranger get between you and the door. Let them take a reasonable look round the unit and chat away about details by the door – unless you have someone with you.

For the gentlemen

If you're showing to single women – open the door and *you* go in first. Leave the front door open again and never let yourself get between a single woman and her exit point. It'll make her feel insecure and could put her off the unit.

Note: if any of this sounds neurotic – I guarantee you're a male reader. Most women learn strategies to keep themselves safe years before they can afford to be landlords.

Once you're both inside

Be friendly but businesslike. This is another clear area of difference in management style between agents and independents. The agent will often send tenants round with a viewer, who only chauffeurs people around and knows nothing about individual properties – let alone tenancy negotiation. The independent landlord will have given real thought to the condition of their property and will have all the answers to questions a tenant might reasonably ask.

Use your common sense. Obviously, the more you like the people in front of you, the more time you'll be inclined to spend. And for those of you who could avoid the HMO legislation by keeping tenant numbers in a unit down to one or two – now is an excellent time to chat through the dim view you'll take of subletting and explain why. It'll only take a moment or two.

The lucky ones among you will have to cut things short for the next appointment, which is also excellent psychology. Explain that you have several appointments (even if you haven't – it gives you a bit of breathing space to think things through). Make sure you have a contact number and tell them you'll let them know later or the following day.

And then? And then nothing. That's a viewing. See, I told you – it's *simple*. Sometimes tenants will take a look and tell you straight away that they are not interested. Don't look offended. Wish them luck in their search and forget about them. Rental property is a horses for courses business and, to double up on clichés, one man's meat is another man's poison.

Reactions from viewing

Sometimes viewers will express an immediate interest. Other times they will make no comment at all. You can't push people into major decisions and both parties giving such a commitment a bit more than ten minutes' consideration is wise. Sometimes, the tenant will be unbelievably enthusiastic, and then you'll never hear from them again!

WARNING ANECDOTE

From my safe viewing chamber of the car, I watched my 6.30 appointment arrive. A skinhead. Covered in tattoos. Bovver boots. Combat pants. No thanks, I decided mentally. But by then another tenant had come into the car park and had stopped to have a chat about the glorious weather, so I couldn't just scarper. Oh yes – this one really was that bad. Knowing someone else was home, someone who'd lived in our unit for years and a burly gent at that, I nodded toward the viewer and did the eye thing. My existing tenant immediately sussed the score. Knew that someone like this would never get a unit from us. He gave me a small nod, then hung around outside the unit waiting for me. Meanwhile, from the safety of the door, I noticed the tea-towel wrapped round my skinhead viewer's fist. And the blood dripping through it onto my freshly cleaned kitchen floor. Slightly unnerved, I mentioned …well…the blood. 'Ah, it n'more'n a scratch love. Want to see some *real* scars?' And he promptly began showing me several of various length on his stubby head. Like I say, explaining that you've other people viewing and that you'll 'let people know by phone tomorrow' can get you out of the oddest of scrapes.

When viewers want you to start removing all your furniture

Some viewers will start asking you to remove all your furniture, or some major parts, say the bed, as they have their own. Defer politely unless you or they are willing to pay for storage – or you have some readily available.

However, if everything goes well – the viewer will express some degree of interest. Keen tenants will ask to be telephoned the next day when you've made your decision. Make sure you remind all interested parties at this stage that you'll be looking for references (by now you need to have chosen which types you're going to ask for) and that you have a Tenancy Application procedure and that successful tenants will need a holding deposit to secure the unit. But maintain viewings until you've secured a Tenant Application Form, cash for the credit/bank checks and a holding deposit.

And with viewings completed, you're now almost a bona fide landlord. Congratulations!

Whys and wherefores

Like much of this guide, this insider knowledge here hasn't been available to new landlords. (Well if it's out there, I certainly haven't found it.) Typing a web search in 'landlord advice' will churn literally hundreds of sites. Few, unfortunately, give much advice on the practicalities.

As for the time conducting viewings will take, that rather depends on the response to your advertising and how you schedule appointments. Reading this lesson itself shouldn't take more than 15–20 minutes. Each viewing will take approximately half an hour of your time, which can *always* be fitted in around a full-time job, as that's exactly what the prospective tenants are doing.

— CHECKLIST/SUMMARY —

■ Arrive early and make your unit look and smell as good as possible – it really helps maximise rent/positive reactions.

▧ Make sure that your unit is furnished unless absolutely necessary – most tenants don't own a van full of furniture and they'll knock your unit to hell moving everything in and out again when they leave.

▧ Put in what's necessary but leave out what won't increase the attractiveness or the rent level.

▧ Ignore advice to fit costly drapes, carpets or kitchens. Make things disposable and attractive. It's a knack worth cultivating. A few weeks' rent doesn't cover much.

▧ Cheap is not shorthand for tacky. Rental units where nothing matches look a mess. You're aiming for 'cheap, durable chic' or 'disposable designer', not dilapidation.

▧ Sit outside in the car (if you can) and watch your appointments arrive. This gives you valuable first reaction time.

▧ Trust your instincts and ask questions that need answering – but don't barrage total strangers.

▧ Run through basic information again. Tenants are often viewing more than one unit in an evening and can get confused.

▧ Don't make instant decisions. Take a phone number and call interested parties later or the following day. If you forget to ask something, this can be an invaluable tool for getting all your questions asked before you decide on anyone.

▧ And yet again, read the whole lesson to get a feel for the process. There's an unwritten rule that tenants who are genuinely interested in a particular property will almost invariably be either early or at worst, on time. Beware the tenant who arrives half an hour late with no apology or extremely good reason – they may try it with the rent.

Lesson 9

Selecting tenants and tying up the deal

Having completed your viewings, go home and think things through. Spur-of-the-moment decisions can often lead to mistakes. If you've never attempted any of this before, review your options.

- Who did you meet?

- Had any of your prospective tenants ever rented before? If so, could they provide that invaluable landlord reference? If not, *why* not?

- Did you prefer any particular viewer above the rest?

- Did they have answers to your questions and provide answers or were they evasive?

- Does anyone who seemed interested strike you as significantly better than the rest?

Experienced tenants know the drill

They know that landlords need certain information and good tenants are up front about providing it. If, on the other hand, they've never rented before, be sure to run through what *you* as a landlord are looking for in terms of prompt rent payment and taking care of the unit before agreeing a tenancy.

Talk to tenants

Choice made, 'jaw jaw is better than war war'. Wise words. This is crunch time. Make sure – especially those of you who are fortunate enough to have units that will be exempt from the new HMO (Houses in Multiple Occupancy) regulations – that you've discussed this no subletting issue with your tenants. Don't be timid or start laying down the law. The overwhelming majority of tenants have *absolutely no idea* of the rules that govern us as landlords. Most, to be blunt don't care either. I have never once in all these years been asked for a copy of a Gas Safety Certificate. Amazing. But this first encounter time is the opportunity to break down some of the barriers. Of course tenants are usually less well-off than landlords. But they can still *speak*, and *hear*. I cannot emphasise enough the importance of building decent relationships and why that matters.

An example

Take a tenant with a job he's had for 18 months, who's lived in your unit and paid on the nose for four months. Then the firm goes bust and he loses his job – through no fault of his own. What do you want:

- an intimidated tenant who doesn't think he can explain his circumstances to you and maybe get a word or two of advice about Housing Benefit;

- someone who will call you immediately because they know you only accept employed tenants and who explains that the Citizens Advice Bureau says he can get Housing Benefit – but it may take weeks to come through?

Personally – I'd go for the second option every time. That way, I get the chance to negotiate. I'd probably say – 'Well okay, thanks for letting me know. I'll wait for the rent to come from Housing Benefit *if* you give me some proof of your claim and I'd like the Housing Benefit cheques to be made out to me direct, so can you ask them for the necessary forms?'

One final consideration

In many ways one of the most important points of all – when will each of the viewers be in a position to move into the unit?

This is really important for landlords trying to fill empty units. Sometimes it can be a fine judgement call indeed between the person your instinct tells you is right – but who hasn't even given his existing landlord notice . . . or the two girls who struck you as a bit flighty but who did offer you an immediate cash deposit to hold the unit, plus they were currently sharing a hotel room and anxious to move in immediately. Ultimately, it's your call. Nevertheless, (very occasionally) that decision will have to be 'no' to everyone you've seen. Re-advertise.

At the end of the day, selecting tenants is a judgement call. Just be certain that however long it takes *you* to decide is a great deal longer than it took the average salesman on commission.

However *don't prevaricate*. The best response you'll ever get is when a unit is freshly advertised when it will hoover up the most likely local candidates. Beyond this initial flurry, you'll often be waiting for stragglers.

A word of warning about references

You have to make checks of some kind, even if your heart (or wallet) is crying out to accept the bloke who seemed okay with a fistful of cash. However, references *can only ever be pieces of paper*. Behind them, there's no security, no comeback. Nor is having a healthy bank balance the same thing as having the intention to pay rent.

Many landlords have come a cropper with the 'loaded' guy with the patter – or that so-sweet librarian with glowing references (including yours truly). So, do what you can to protect yourself without being so cautious that you lose a perfectly good tenant. Bank/employer references can only ever say so much. The ideal reference is a verifiable one from a former landlord (if you can check it's not someone's best friend).

Beware of professional shysters

Out there are some full-time crooks/tenants who operate in rentals. Some go to tremendous lengths to consolidate their 'stings'. And, where they also affect us independents (who have the limited protection of their gut instincts) – they seem to prefer the anonymity of agents. References can be forged. Utility bills can be appropriated from friends/empty units they've previously viewed. Below shows just how far some scoundrels can go.

WARNING ANECDOTE

The *Guardian* recently reported a terrifying tenant fraud. Living abroad in his mortgage-free house, the owner handed over the property to an agent. A tenant was found, who produced deposits and the necessary documentation to set up a lease. He never moved in. Instead, having changed the utility bills to his (false) name – he promptly – posing as the owner – managed to obtain a £200,000 mortgage against the property.

Eventually the owner got his property back – and the lender was left trying to track down the fraudster. Now obviously, this is an extreme case. But it shows just how vulnerable landlords can be in a climate where identity fraud is growing fast. I routinely collect and return to sender any uncollected mail from tenants who've left. Heaven only knows how easy it is to steal identity when no one from the managing agency ever visits rented property to clear mail.

Rental virgins

Young tenants often simply don't realise how expensive leaving home can be. But again I repeat – whoever you let to, there's little to beat a system where you select your own tenants and let them know that you'll be visiting to collect rent personally each month/week or whatever. I know it sounds involved but it works. Everything else is simply trying to replicate less effective versions of the above. Non-payers and party animals usually prefer the anonymity of the agent whose property management department (which knows they're in arrears) is miles away, and doesn't know them from Adam. It's also tremendously difficult for tenants who've agreed in writing to your rent collection visits to complain that you're 'harassing them' if you turn up more than once – a regular occurrence from tenants whose agent never goes near the place if the landlord has the temerity to knock on their door and ask what's happening to the rent.

Credit checks

Whoever you ultimately choose, you'd be reckless not to carry out a *credit check*. Every financial move we make nowadays is monitored and even the lowest paid people will have some form of credit history. If *any* problems show up – walk away. You don't ever want to house a debtor.

Employer references can also be taken, unless you are one of those landlords who will accept the unemployed on Housing Benefit.

However, never kid yourself that anything on paper can do more than *lower* your risks. Letting is never a risk-free business.

Decision time

Unless I've scared you to death, now's the time to decide which interested party comes top of your list and call them first. If they're still interested, make an appointment to meet as soon as practicable to exchange some monies and fill in documents. Your next move must be to meet one of the interested parties (and try calling your second preference for a fall-back position).

With you, at this second meeting, you'll need Tenant Application Form(s) and Parental Guarantor Form(s) – where applicable – plus a receipt book with duplicates (available from any stationers).

The time for signing leases comes *after* references have been checked, never before.

Tenant Application Forms and Parental Guarantor Forms

It's now time to ask your tenant (or tenants) to complete a Tenant Application Form(s) (remember one form per tenant, so take enough) or a Parental Guarantor Form (for young tenants). Run through the details and point out the small reference charges (ask for payment there and then). Cheques for this amount of money are usually accompanied by a cheque guarantee card and should be fine – but cash is better eight days a week.

Holding deposit

Once you have completed Tenancy Application Forms, you'll need a holding deposit. This should be for at least one week's rent and you cannot proceed on uncleared cheques. Explain why. Some tenants will disappear for a short time to the nearest cash point. Others will want to let the cheque clear first – a less than ideal situation that may make you reconsider your options. Most astute tenants know the score and – if funds exist – anyone working should be able to withdraw £200–£250 within a short time. If funds are so tight that the tenant is waiting for a pay-cheque to clear – ask yourself how this is all going to work when you'll need the balance of the deposit and a full month's rent. Another judgement call. If you're down to a choice of one tenant – carry on – accept the cheque and bank it immediately – but *don't* arrange moving-in day and lease signing until that cheque has cleared. Tenants insisting on cheques need to pay you the balance of the deposit plus all advance rent at least a week before the moving-in day – and always check that funds have cleared before signing *any* leases. They can't be unsigned – remember that fixed term?

WARNING ANECDOTE

This story was reported in the *Observer* (January 2007). Having advertised a unit at what looked like below cost, a landlord took holding deposits of a month's rent. In return, he gave a receipt showing that the tenancy was subject to satisfactory references at a rate of £75 each plus costs. In the end, the bar of 'satisfactory' seemed to be set rather high. The complaining tenants received a refund of a mere £200 from their original £900. Chelsea Citizens Advice Bureau at Chelsea Town Hall is reported as having more cases involving the same 'references' issue since September 2006 with the same individual. No wonder tenants are nervy creatures.

Money talk

Money talk is alien to some people. But the *only* reason that you're a private landlord is to generate money and you need to learn *fast* how to discuss the very reason you're all standing around in the unit.

A holding deposit is just what it says on the tin. An agreement not to let the unit to anyone else unless there's a problem with some of the references. It's an interim stage. Be patient. This is a long-haul agreement lasting months, possibly years – getting things right often takes a few days.

What to put on the receipt

Holding deposits are informal pre-contractual agreements between strangers bound up by money. Ensure that you write on the receipt that the holding deposit *is non-refundable should references/credit checks prove unsatisfactory or if the tenant changes their mind about wanting the unit known as . . .* [insert address, date and sign]. Unless you do this – if the tenant changes their mind or has lousy references – they'll be fully entitled to a refund and you're left with nothing.

What happens to the holding deposit?

Explain again that this sum will be deducted from the remaining deposit required for the rental. For example, tenants renting a unit for £100 per week will need a deposit of four (or six) week's rent (never more, see Lesson 10 on deposits – you'll create a premium). This means their total deposit will be £400. Thus the minimum holding deposit should be £100, leaving a deposit balance outstanding of £300. This holding deposit has the specific purpose of covering the landlord's losses if references don't stack up or if tenants change their minds. It is *not* additional pocket money for dodgy landlords.

What if someone better comes along or I change my mind about the tenant whose holding deposit I've taken? Refund the first tenant in full if *you* change your mind.

Anything else?

But of course, there's bound to be a bit of work involved with making thousands of pounds over the lifetime of a rental.

So, once you're home with your Tenant Application Forms and holding deposits get on with the referencing process.

Get cracking because time equals money to landlords. Telephone a company for credit references (*Yellow Pages*). Make whatever checks you've decided are essential as quickly as possible by phone, fax, email or snail mail.

And finally – assuming everything is fine with references and checks and you have your guarantor forms back, notify your tenant of the happy news. It is unwise to accept Parental Guarantees from companies unless you can check trading accounts via Companies House.

Then what?

Either:

1. Set up a meeting to accept the remainder of the deposit and advance rent, which will begin the formalities of a tenancy and will only be complete and binding once leases have been signed and witnessed.

Or:

2. (My personal preference), wait until the agreed moving-in date and (so long as cash is available for the remainder of the deposit and the one month's advance rent) complete all the formalities (exchange of money, inventory, schedule of condition and leases) in one go on the first day of the tenancy. And *always* take a witness.

Each scenario suits different landlords and I've little doubt there are other permutations of the process that suit individuals better. Some landlords prefer to only accept cheques for security reasons and therefore have to work a full week ahead of themselves in order to allow cheques to clear. Others are quite happy to cut down appointments and accept cash. Yet again, it's your call. There's only one rule and it's simple. *Never* complete the formalities of a tenancy, let alone hand over keys to a property, without some credit reference and the full amount of genuine money.

Some ideas for all those forms you'll need to use

There's no common format for reference forms or for Tenancy Application Forms and no real need to buy them. Overleaf are examples of forms I use and which have served me perfectly well. Copy them if you like – or pay someone to draw up something similar. But please don't try managing without any of them because checks like these are a vital part of your own protection against wilful damage or neglect. You need to decide which forms apply and when to use them appropriately. So, every tenant gets a Tenant Application Form, but obviously a 30 year old won't be providing parental guarantors – unless their parents are very understanding. And, in case you don't have details of how to compile one, there's also a sample employment reference included in this Lesson.

And finally, for bank references

Most major banks have a standard form of reference. Please refer to your Tenant Application Form for account details then ring the relevant contact and ask what they will require/provide.

Tying up the deal before moving tenants into a unit

Assuming you're doing everything on moving-in day and the unit is prepared:

1. Agree a moving-in date and time with new tenants.

2. Meet up, enter the unit and go through the inventory and Schedule of Condition in detail with your tenant. Anything added in at this stage is likely to be handwritten so please get your tenants to initial and date any changes. Show them a *current* Landlord's Gas Safety Certificate (unless there's no gas in the building).

3. Now we come to money. Tenants should have the balance of the deposit and a full month's advance rent. Don't accept excuses here – it's sheer madness to start off a brand new tenancy any other way – instead really consider whether or not you want them as tenants at all – as this is a very bad first impression.

Full name...

National Insurance or passport number ....

Current address...
....

Previous address (if you've lived at your current address for less than three years, please provide all other addresses for that period)
....
....

Where are you currently registered for Council Tax? (students may provide parental home) ....

Name, address and telephone number of previous landlord ....
....

Employer ....

How long have you worked for this employer? ....

Your starting date at this employer ....

If less than three years, please give details of other employers during the last three years...
....

Are you paid weekly? YES ☐ NO ☐

Are you paid calendar monthly? YES ☐ NO ☐

Please give details of your bank (please note, building society passbooks are *not* accepted) including account details, sort code and full postal address of bank
....

Do you authorise a reference from your bank? YES ☐ NO ☐

Do you authorise a full credit check? YES ☐ NO ☐

The cost for each of the above is £10. Will you pay these referencing costs in advance? YES ☐ NO ☐

Personal details

Date of birth..

Character referees (please provide two if no landlord reference is available)
....
....

Name and telephone number of next of kin (for emergencies only)
....

Signature of tenant .... Date........................

A parental guarantor is required for all tenants under 25 years of age. Please give name and address of a person who will act as guarantor ....
....

Please note:

1 It is the policy of this landlord to pursue all debts to County Court Judgements.

2 Deposit returns are made within 10 days of vacating the premises in cheque form and to an accurate forwarding address only.

Guidelines for Tenant Application Form

Full name...

Full postal address ....

....

Previous address (if you've lived here for less than three years)...........

....

Where are you currently registered for Council Tax?......................

....

Full name of person whom you are providing a financial parental guarantee for...

Their date of birth ....

State your relationship ....

Please read the following and sign only if you agree all parts of the following statement, completing on the dotted lines where appropriate:

I (please state full name) ....

of (your address) ....

....

hereby agree to act as financial guarantor for (please state name of party you're acting as guarantor for here.....................................

for the duration of their tenancy on the property known as (name of rental address)...

....

for the entire duration of the said tenancy. I hereby underwrite full financial responsibility for all unpaid rent, unsettled bills and for all damage to the property and contents arising as a consequence of this tenancy both during and after the said tenancy between (name of tenant)..

and

(name of landlord) ....

within 14 days of such demand from the landlord. I confirm receipt of the copy Inventory and Schedule of Condition and accept them as accurate and binding.

Please sign here..

Date...

Please return this completed form to me as soon as possible. Thank you.

[Name and address of landlord] ....

....

....

Guidelines and suggestions for Parental Guarantor Form

Dear (please insert company contact name)

Tenant's name and job title

....

The above named has applied to rent a property from me and has given your details as their employer. The applicant has declared their salary on their Tenant Application Form and has given written permission for me to verify this information.

I would be very grateful if you could provide the following:

1. Confirmation of their employment start date

....

2. Confirm their job title

....

3. Confirm whether this position is part or full time

....

Has a permanent post YES ☐ NO ☐

Or has a contract YES ☐ NO ☐

If contract, please confirm duration of such contract

....

Please confirm their gross annual income....................................

Or hourly rate..

Regular overtime or bonus payments...

Any additional comments...

....

....

Your name ....

Position..

Signed..

Dated...

Company stamp if available

In order that I process this information toward their tenancy, I'd be grateful if you could return this form immediately to myself at the following address or fax me direct on 0208 949 6476.

Lesley Henderson
67 XXX Road,
Wimbledon SW18 4HY

Yours sincerely

Example of an employment reference

4. Assuming (as in the overwhelming majority of cases) that the money is available, provide two receipts, one showing the balance of the deposit paid which states 'balance of outstanding deposit', and another separate receipt for rent, which states 'rent for –' and provide the first and last day of the period covered (usually four weeks apart) and the address of the unit. Sign and date one then give one copy to the tenants and keep your duplicates. Alternatively rent books for assured shorthold tenancies are available from many stationers for around £1.50.

5. Now run through the lease (unless you've already shown them at any previous meetings). Encourage them to read it and, especially for units with one or two tenants, point out the subletting restrictions and explain why this is so important – especially with the new HMO legislation and *make sure they understand*.

6. If they don't seem overly interested in the paperwork, that's up to them. Tenants are split pretty much down the middle over these matters. Either they check each comma or they don't bother to read it at all. If it's 30 pages long, I hope you forewarned them and brought a good novel if they're the interested type.

7. Fill in both leases (see Lesson 5: Assured shorthold leases) one copy for yourself and one for your new tenant. Sign them and ask your tenant to sign them. Date them, then have them witnessed.

8. Some landlords still collect rent, sometimes weekly, sometimes fortnightly but more often, four weekly. Many tenants and landlords however, prefer to have standing order arrangements via the tenant's bank. The choice for this is for the landlord to make and the tenant to oblige. If you require a standing order, make sure that you have ordered or collected one from the bank for this first day and get the tenant to fill it in before you hand over the keys. Some landlords prefer a combination where, say for the first three months, they meet the tenant and collect rent, then set up bank arrangements once they're confident a payment pattern will continue. Others simply plump for one method or the other. There are, as usual, benefits and drawbacks to both methods. Some landlords opting for standing orders/direct debits sensibly arrange

with their own bank to have statements sent out *immediately post rent dates*. It's a very interesting argument – often hotly disputed between independents. Very few people manage to get into arrears with rent collection and interestingly, WH Smith always carries healthy stocks of appropriate rent books so plenty of landlords must still opt for it.

Rent collection services

Set this up from day one and tell your tenants exactly when to expect you. Tenants who run into arrears find it easy to avoid the local lettings agent and an absent landlord. They're much less likely to want to face the landlord in person. Leaving a note to say you'll be back tomorrow at the same time can nip an escalating problem of repeated non-payment in the bud.

Rocks and hard places

As a landlord you can get stuck in a number of them until you refine your practice to suit your circumstances and the nature of your units. Being an independent allows you to intervene effectively and early – it's another significant benefit that shouldn't be given up lightly.

And finally

Leave the tenants a Property Profile. Once at home, telephone the local authority council tax office and provide them with the details of your new tenant who will be responsible for charges from their first day. Water companies will need similar notification (even if the water is metered). Tenants will need to be advised who the gas and electricity suppliers are so that bills can be put in their names – these days tenants swap and change suppliers all the time. But sensible landlords take meter readings to protect themselves and their tenants. I always write mine in the bottom left corner of the lease, that way, when a company tries to back bill your new tenant for the old tenants arrears, you're all quite certain what the meter said on day one.

Whys and wherefores

Selecting tenants is time well spent. How long all this takes is a matter of the variables. Reading the lesson (which itself shouldn't take more than 20 minutes or so), this part of the process may sound daunting, but don't be put off. What I can say with confidence is that after the first or second time, doing anything connected to with letting only takes a matter of minutes or an odd hour – it's just that the unfamiliar can take a bit of getting used to.

Referencing tenants is one of the topics covered widely on the internet landlord sites, such as the Small Landlords Association, the Residential Landlord Association and the Royal Institute of Chartered Surveyors sites, who may have ideas not covered here. Other information is available through the multiple landlord sites that have mushroomed recently. Experian (tel: 0870 241 6212) (for £10 credit references) and Credit PLC (tel: 0870 060 1414). Other suppliers of credit and other referencing service like Equifax and *www.tenantvetting.org.uk* are available online.

Alternatively, *Yellow Pages* lists tenant vetting services and credit checking companies.

– CHECKLIST/SUMMARY –

- Go home after meeting prospective tenants and give the matter some genuine thought.

- Leave your prejudices behind, being discriminatory is illegal and poor business.

- Make sure you remember when each person will be able to move in.

- Trust your judgement but check whatever is checkable.

- Don't be indecisive, the first flurry of tenants is usually the best.

- Make your decision and telephone the tenants to arrange a second meeting.

- Discuss holding deposits and Tenant Application Forms when tenants call.

- Don't discard telephone numbers of other interested parties yet – you might need a fall-back position.

■ If other interested viewers telephone you to ask whether or not they've been successful, use the first come, first served reasoning and tell them you'll be in touch if the tenant backs out or proves unsatisfactory.

■ References are only pieces of paper – don't be over reliant on them.

■ Always do a credit check – they're easy, cheap and quick and screen out persistent debtors.

■ Ask tenants to pay a combined fee of around £20–£25 for both bank and credit references when they complete Tenant Application Forms (they'll know this is fair – it's a good way to start a new business relationship).

■ Notice what's on the bottom of my Tenant Application Forms. One clause will be explained in the deposits lesson, the other is self-explanatory.

■ Always insist on a holding deposit of at least one week's rent. If you don't get a holding deposit from your first choice, ask yourself why and move to your second preference. Never stop advertising until you've taken some money on a unit.

■ Always provide receipts for holding deposits with clear terms.

■ Make sure the receipt states clearly what the money is for and, in the case of a holding deposit, that it may prove non-refundable.

■ When checking references, try to speed things up with phone calls and faxes – but ask people to fill in the forms for your records. Electoral Registers can confirm old address details for example.

■ If your tenant's references are not satisfactory, don't proceed – grit your teeth and start again!

■ Read the whole of this lesson – much of it is very important.

Lesson 10

Deposits

If ever there was a great idea that got 'lost in translation' – it's good old rental deposits. Moreover, as landlords, don't *ever* expect to be given the benefit of the doubt by tenants (or proud parents of); to say nothing of courts, sadly our track record just doesn't stand up to scrutiny. More than ten per cent of full rental deposits evaporate each year – to say nothing of inflated or unfair deductions from the remaining 90 per cent. You do the sums. This an awful lot of cash to go walkies without any accountability.

So, under new legislation which came into force on 6 April 2007, landlords and agents are legally obliged to safeguard all tenancy deposits (on assured shortholds). And this legislation means business!

What's all the fuss about?

In principle, deposits were the perfect device to protect landlords from the abuse of their property. Unfortunately, though this is pretty blunt and doesn't apply to the majority, there's been so much chicanery and plain and simple theft by landlords and agents it's beyond excuses. Legislation came into force from 6 April 2007 – and this legislation has teeth. Landlords who fail to comply can lose their rights to shorthold possession in courts – thus the whole *principle* that underpins assured shortholds is lost – for non-compliance. There are also significant financial penalties for refusing to act lawfully under these new rules.

No landlord is legally allowed to take and hold any new tenancy deposit whatsoever on *any* assured shorthold tenancy unless they comply with the following (and I quote the legislation here):

1. A landlord must deal with the deposit in accordance with an *authorised* Scheme (in other words must make sure that the

tenant's deposit is safeguarded by one of the three main Schemes – more details later in the Lesson).

2. Landlords/agents must comply with the initial requirements of that chosen Scheme *within 14 days* (again, more details on where to find these Schemes later in the Lesson).

3. Landlords *must provide the tenant* with 'the appropriate' information relating to the said Scheme within 14 days of receiving the deposit from the tenant.

(Wherever the word 'landlord' is used, this term also encompasses *any third parties* – including but not exclusive to letting/estate agents – ie no shenanigans will be allowed to circumvent this particular law.)

Until all these specific procedures (explained later in this Lesson) have been put in place by the landlord or their agents, applications for possession under Section 21 (after the initial fixed term has expired) *will not be accepted by courts* on any tenancy initiated after 6 April 2007, where landlords/agents have failed to act lawfully.

Other consequences of landlords failing to comply

Beyond the possession issue, tenants have other sanctions against landlords who fail to comply with the law after 6 April 2007 that courts can enforce:

1. Tenants can apply to the court to force the landlord to repay the deposit – if it is not protected by a Scheme.

2. If landlords still fail to act as instructed – courts can award tenants three times the original deposit, payable within 10 days, by way of sanction.

The situation on the ground

However, before we tackle the new legislation itself, let's do some real spadework that will apply to either the old or new systems and try learning how to avoid problems in the first place. Many of us will be holding rental deposits on tenancies established before April 2007 for quite some time, ie possibly for several years, therefore both old and new systems are likely to be operating side by side until all pre-April 2007 tenancies eventually conclude. Given the scale of funds involved (ie tens of millions of pounds) – many existing landlords will have to learn to juggle both systems for quite a while yet – so understanding how to manage deposits becomes one of the only areas of landlord management to come under official scrutiny that we have to confront. Getting this aspect of management right *matters*. What's more, getting it wrong is no longer an option. Learning how to assess things fairly becomes a vital landlord skill after April 2007.

Landlords need to learn how to manage all *tenancy deposits fairly*

Not only has the handling of rental deposits been widely abused, the mutual trust necessary to make them work well has also disappeared. Cowboys and cheats have terminally tainted everyone.

(Remember my tale of cleaning costs at £125 per hour?) Nor was that in any way unique. Some landlords/agents have been routinely charging astronomical amounts of money from fairly powerless tenants then cranking up costs with 'administration fees' – greed is never a pretty sight.)

So, let's be quite clear. After 6 April 2007 landlords/agents lost the right to autonomously decide on any deposit deductions *that aren't agreed in* advance *with their tenants*.

In *all* cases of dispute, a third party will become involved by law. In other words, both landlords *and* tenants are going to have to learn to negotiate together. Stamping feet, yelling and refusing to accept responsibility will be futile because *every case of dispute* on a tenancy created after 6 April 2007 will now be managed by either Alternative Dispute Resolution (ADR) or by the courts – if *either* landlord or tenant won't agree to use dispute resolution. A landlord/agent's former autonomy is gone. Everything now depends on negotiated agreements or imposed settlements by others. In other words, big changes all round. And if it's all making your head spin a bit, trust me, you're certainly not alone!

Because the ink is still damp as I type and things have been added to the information database each time I go online, I can't be as detailed as I would have liked about precisely how the new Schemes will operate. Like you, I just have my fingers crossed and am hoping for the best. However, learning how to manage both the old and new systems simultaneously is now part and parcel of being a modern landlord. Welcome to the new transparent world of deposit management.

To make life easier, I intend trying to show you what is and isn't a reasonable mindset to apply to deposits under either system. That way, either now or under the most demanding new legislation, you shouldn't go too far wrong. To achieve this, I've split the remainder of this lesson into two parts.

1. How to manage any rental deposit – irrespective of the system in force.

2. A brief outline of the options a landlords has for the legal safeguarding of all new tenants' deposits from 6 April 2007, plus access to (a great deal of) further information that you can rely on.

Part 1: How to manage any rental deposit

Under any system, the deposit concept is simple. Landlords (or agents) ask for a deposit of money as a modest financial guarantee that care will be taken of the landlord's property and lease obligations are met. Then, if tenants cause damage, don't clear up adequately, leave the unit with bills outstanding – or a multitude of other scenarios too numerous to list – the landlord has some form of financial fall-back.

How much to deduct has previously been in the hands of landlords and agents, leaving tenants who felt ripped off with no option but the courts to challenge excessive charges or exaggerated damages. This all changes on tenancies created after April 2007. However, reasonable costings still need to be negotiated under the new Schemes as well as the old system. Learning what is and isn't a fair deduction simply becomes more open after April 2007 as independent overseers will become involved in debates over charges disputed by tenants, where

Schemes are involved. Learning what will and won't be acceptable to Schemes and courts thus becomes a real requirement to avoid protracted disputes.

Who deposits always belong to – irrespective of systems

Rental deposits always remain the tenant's money, simply held 'just in case'.

Let tenants know that you respect this. Remember the psychology. Don't give new tenants any excuses to behave badly – they *may* just take them. You also need to clearly establish – from day one, both now and under the new rules – just exactly how a tenant needs to re-present the property at the end of their tenancy in order to get a full deposit refund.

A well returned unit and a *full* deposit refund always was and always will be the *ideal situation* to aim for, especially under the new rules.

Some parts of the letting's roller-coaster have become over reliant on end of lease charging. The new legislation should end this.

Laughing yet?
Well you shouldn't be. This is good, old-fashioned *tenant management* – lost as tenants became soft targets under legislation that has effectively left them powerless. It simply isn't fair to overcharge tenants just because you think you can get away with it – end of topic. Trust me, that win-win situation I repeatedly mention really does make the contract work better for *both* parties. Tenants are not cash cows to be endlessly milked. Landlords/agents don't have 'rights' to deduct money now, they never did, and new laws will prevent it from happening from now on. Nor can we use other people's cash to refurbish units instead of paying out for routine maintenance. This is 'wear and tear'. Landlords already have a tax allowance for this.

Deposits are only ever available to cover *reasonable* charges for *unreasonable* actions.

Besides which, tenants *don't* laugh. I've seen them reduced to tears over outrageous deductions charged by some colleagues. Remember those people skills? You have to learn to understand your customers. And their financial realities. So, let's learn how to do things fairly – then, whichever laws apply – you should steer clear of trouble.

It's easy to get it right

■ Make sure that your unit is presented properly in the first place – even the cheapest units should be reasonable and must always be safe.

■ Get it cleaned.

■ Make a *detailed* Inventory and a Schedule. Get them signed by tenants as a fair record of how things were presented on moving-in day and always keep your copies safe.

■ Take some digital photos and get the tenants to sign and date them too as an additional record.

■ And, *most importantly*, talk to your tenants. Remember, this is a big financial transaction on both sides. It can't be shuffled through in a couple of minutes because both parties are too embarrassed to talk about the contract realities or can't make time to bother.

■ For any tenancy created after April 2007 choose a Scheme provider and follow their rules for deposit control (read the whole Lesson for fuller details of your options under the new rules).

■ Let your tenants know which Scheme you are using and explain that documentation will reach them shortly giving them formal notice of precisely which Scheme is safeguarding their deposit.

Always walk new tenants around on moving-in day and explain exactly how you'll expect the unit to be returned. Point out a few examples. The clean walls. The spotless oven. Make it plain that their deposit will be fully refunded if the property is left as found.

Make it crystal clear that a full deposit refund is your *ideal* scenario.

If you have evidence, show them receipts for other full deposit returns provided in the past, to reassure them. Believe me, these things can make a great deal of difference to trust levels.

Under new or old systems, you should make it clear from the outset that any moving-out inspection cannot take place before tenants have left and returned the keys. None of these scenarios is altered by the new legislation. Both parties have their interests to protect and many landlords will continue to hold rental deposits, almost exactly as before (see Part 2 for Scheme provider options). Only the *manner* in which refunds are resolved and *accounted for* will change on leases created after April 2007.

I do know kindly landlords who fall into the trap of paying out on leaving day and it's very understandable, tenants often need one deposit back to fund the next. However, it's simply impossible to assess a returned property unless you have half an hour's peace and quiet to run through your own Inventory and Schedule without someone breathing down your neck. It certainly doesn't happen with agencies. There's no reason why independent landlords should feel obliged to act instantaneously either. If you want to help your tenant quickly, you can always invite them back, say later that same evening, to sort out deposit returns.

(Again, I emphasise, deposit *refunds* will often be largely unaffected by the new Schemes – they're being introduced to control unfair *deductions*. Landlords will still retain the option of holding deposits, whilst simultaneously having them safeguarded by a Scheme. What's introduced is simply a new layer of paperwork, created to prevent outrageous deductions that have become too commonplace.)

What's more usual than any instantaneous cash deposit refund is to remind tenants of the clear statement on their Tenant Application Form that you cannot return cash over a pile of boxes, applicable in all but the most exceptional of circumstances. Again, this is a situation which will not be altered one jot by the April 2007 legislation.

Sending a deposit refund cheque through the post has consistently proved to be the only way that any landlord/agent could realistically track down tenants who left a trail of bad debts behind which would adversely affect the next tenants who tried to live there in peace. It's remains a good idea for those reasons so stick to it wherever you can. Don't feel pressurised to respond like a hole in the wall on moving-out day, but don't hold on to deposits due for return either. New rules insist on deposit returns within ten days. However that's the new legal maximum. In my experience, matters can be easily checked and verified to allow cheques to be in the post within 48 hours.

Return deposit balances promptly

When tenants genuinely do return a unit in good condition and you've checked their bill status – post their cheque immediately (or inform the appropriate Scheme promptly if you've chosen the Custodial Option – see Part 2). Fairness will give you the type of track record that tenants are looking for. And a good local track record attracts new tenants like a magnet. Besides, tenants are customers, not chattels. If you want to lord it over someone, get a dog.

But you should hear my horror stories!

Oh, but I *have*. And I've had fair my share of units trashed. And my share of likeable young men who lived like hogs. But they were a tiny minority and you can't base a business philosophy on minorities. If you (or your agent) are repeatedly attracting the type of tenants who trash property then I'm afraid that there is something fundamentally wrong with either your presentation, property condition or your management style. So if your tenants are always the troublemakers, start wondering why and try changing something.

Most tenants try very hard to make sure they return property nicely because they *need* that deposit back.

Trust is a precarious thing. It needs to be built where such expensive assets are being exchanged for something as small as one rent payment at a time. The last thing you need is a tenant with access to a valuable asset, who genuinely believes that your sole aim in life is to bleed them dry. They may well find ways to return the compliment.

Deduct only what's fair

No matter how badly any tenant has behaved you're still only entitled to deduct the *true cost* of the remedial work they created a need for. Because they made you angry doesn't give you the right to surcharge them, no matter how tempting that can be when you're furious. And of course, the new legislation is now in place precisely to prevent abuse – so be very wary about temper tariffs.

Deposits can be a vicious circle – or a virtuous one. New systems will only force bad landlords to change their conduct. Good landlords/agents will find little changes but the papertrail.

For those landlords who have used an independent inventory service, simply make an appointment for the end of tenancy check-out. Make certain that any required costs are clear as the new Schemes will require these documents in any case of dispute. For the majority of you with your own Inventories and Schedules, please read on for some practical advice – applicable both now and after April 2007. I stress, only the system you are obliged to choose will change, not the responsibility of tenants for damage.

What can I reasonably charge for under either system?

Let's take a look at damage, something that all landlords need to learn how to assess fairly under any deposit system.

(Landlords can expect from the old and new systems either a repair cost where one is required, or, if something is genuinely ruined or broken, the true costs of replacement. However, that *doesn't* mean an upgrade. Nor does it mean charging tenants for things that have simply worn out or which were too cheap to withstand wear and tear – ie normal usage.)

Broken furniture, for example, is easy enough to prove, agree and calculate. However, it's the other forms of damage or abuse that cause most conflict. Most of these situations will, under the new laws, need to be discussed and costs agreed with tenants. Where agreement cannot be reached, one of the new Schemes will have to become involved by law (read Part 2). Unfortunately, things are often not so cut and dried as a broken chair – something, I suspect, the new arbitrators are about to discover.

Sometimes, tenants spill things (especially, for some inexplicable reason on carpets and beds). So let's see what could be a reasonable approach here.

■ If it can be cleaned, then the cost of cleaning should be acceptable under any system, old or new – so long as you have receipts for proof of the cost.

■ When things go beyond a general clean and require specialist equipment or even replacement, get estimates then discuss matters urgently with your former tenants. Carpets are a particularly contentious area (actually a filthy carpet can look pretty similar to a clean one in a photo). Nor do they always clean up well when dirt is ground in or when badly stained. In some instances, a replacement really is called for.

■ However, if tenants don't agree with your decision or costings, start to take precautions to protect yourself. This is dispute territory – under both old and *especially* under the new systems.

■ Make sure you have damage/dirt authenticated by a witness or, at the very least take digital photos to compare with your originals before you replace anything using someone else's money (a decision you'll be unable to legally take without your tenant's consent under the new system – see Part 2).

Then, there are bed issues. Okay, I can see an explanation for the coffee cup tipping but I can honestly admit that the state of some mattresses can make you gasp. No court nor Scheme (so long as you have photographic proof) can ask you to get a mattress cleaned – it will need to be replaced. (Tip – always remove mattress covers and inspect both sides, tenants have a tendency to simply turn them over to conceal stains.)

■ If any dispute is ongoing, buy a new mattress and get money reimbursed later – you need to keep your business running. Under the new Schemes, this may apply to quite a lot of things or landlords would end up with empty units for weeks on end until arbitration/courts have come to decisions over relatively trivial amounts – a situation that simply doesn't make business sense.

■ Get receipts for every penny you spend whatever the legal position (costs like these may well be tax deductible).

Other common problems

Cigarette burns are remarkably common. Many landlords try to avoid this by insisting on non-smoking tenants, however, this is simply impractical to police. For a single burn in a corner, a small deduction or maybe even a rug could be reasonably expected. For a single burn slap bang in the middle of a brand new cream carpet, you may feel justified in expecting far more. For numerous careless burns all over the place you can now – and always will be – well within your rights to expect a new carpet to be fitted. Only the *way* in which landlords proceed will change, not the principal behind tenant responsibilities. Tenants are *always* liable for damage they cause, whatever the system.

Other types of damage

Loss or theft: if it was on the Inventory and a tenant signed for it, she or he is responsible for the replacement cost of *equivalent* missing items.

Spoiled decorations: this is another common area of dispute. Dirty walls need washing down – tenants either do this before they move or expect to be charged the full economic cost of cleaning up (I always use a bucket of hot washing soda and rubber gloves). Get receipts for everything – you need to prove costs under either system. The same applies to those beer stains on the ceiling (remember that Schedule of Condition I suggested that you draw up . . .?).

A few extra chips on paintwork is almost inevitable as people move into and out of units and is wear and tear. Wholesale lumps gouged from every door frame and skirting board is not. Burns on loo cisterns or worse, on the side of the immaculate plastic bath, are very expensive to sort out and absolutely not acceptable either. Neither is the sash window tenants 'forgot' to mention they broke months ago.

The fittings

Landlords vary widely about the standard of their facilities. Sensible ones buy robust kitchen cupboards and worktops – decent drawers, etc. Others will provide shoddy quality. This is the stuff of any landlord/court/arbitrators nightmares.

- If the kitchen cupboards have cheap hinges and the doors fall off, you can hardly blame a tenant.

- On the other hand, if tenants have mistreated a perfectly good kitchen cupboard, they should expect to be billed for repairs.

- Likewise, a badly joined worktop will deteriorate fast and is not the tenants' problem.

- But a decent worktop, repeatedly used as a chopping board, most certainly is.

(Because kitchens are costly and fitting out rentals has to be practical, I always recommend reasonable kitchens, which come with a ten-year guarantee. Most large DIY stores offer something like this, so spending a fortune is not necessary or indeed, even desirable for average rentals. That way, the standard of what is normal wear and tear is established by the company guarantee – making disputes easier to settle.)

Where things get trickier

How to deal with dirt and grime
This is often a much stickier wicket ('scuse the pun). No matter how clean they can appear in themselves, some tenants' idea of 'clear up' comes nowhere close to as good as on acceptance. Indeed, it's ironic that the clean presentation that attracted them in the first place is often the last thing they expect to replicate when they move out!

Fifty per cent of tenants that I've housed over 35 years simply don't clean behind the loo or scour out the oven and defrost fridges/freezers. I'd estimate that 90 per cent fail to hoover under beds, no matter how thoroughly I explain in advance.

These issues are quite hard to prove especially when relying on photos and inventories. An independent witness is always better than simply relying on paper records and photos. It's also quite impossible to photograph a smell – sometimes the first warning of major steam cleaning requirements. Again, that judgement call. Make sure that your unit is cleaned up and get things back up to scratch before new tenants move in. However, while you're left in charge of old deposits, do bill at a reasonable local rate for the job, not some extortionate rate plucked from thin air. It can and often will be challenged – and quite right too.

Note: please don't imagine that the new Tenancy Deposit Scheme is a one-way ticket against landlords. Many reasonable landlords have had real trouble with tenants who refuse to accept responsibility for anything. Quite soon, tenants too will have to take a view on reasonable deductions and charges – or risk tying up some or all of their deposit for quite some time in a Scheme.

But how will I prove any of these scenarios?

Landlords who have their management ducks in a row already have a great deal of evidence for a court or any adjudicator of a Scheme. You have paperwork: signed comprehensive Inventories, signed Schedules of Condition, possibly signed photographs, signed leases, which incorporate your rights as well as your tenants', and probably a suitcase full of receipts to show how much things cost and how old they are. These show a responsible mindset and all you then need are either new photos or a witness who will back you up or preferably both. (Note: a willing next-door neighbour can often make an invaluable impartial witness – learning how to be friendly with the person next door is an invaluable landlord skill definitely worth cultivating.)

Reinforcing the cleanliness message

Remember my insistence on reinforcing cleanliness throughout the Inventory and Schedule of Condition? Tenants can't give things a quick wipe and expect you to do deep cleaning for free, assuming some kind of miraculous *quid pro quo*. But they often try to, which is why I set aside a few minutes in the final month to remind them how clean the unit was on acceptance. No misunderstandings that way – though they rarely listen hard enough to remember under the beds.

When tenants leave owing rent

Obviously, if your tenant owes you rent, you're entitled to expect repayment from deposits. I see no reason that the appearance of a tenant's deposit scheme will alter most of these scenarios one jot – all you'll need is proof of non-payment – hardly difficult to provide for landlords who keep records.

Unfortunately, once all the deposit has been used up to cover back rent, this can leave landlords with no money left to cover other, quite genuine repairs and cleaning. This is not part of the Tenancy Deposit Scheme's remit, but becomes small claims court time for landlords (see Lesson 11 on ending leases). Courts are not just for ill-treated tenants – they're there to help you too. It can all be done online these days and isn't at all complicated. If you're confused, ring your local court. They won't give you legal advice but they will tell you how to complete applications properly. Don't just allow tenants to run off owing you a small fortune and do nothing. Besides, a County Court Judgement helps forewarn future landlords about potentially trouble-some tenants on our credit checks...so hey... do us all a favour!

Unpaid bills

Utility bills are an absolute must for landlords on all check-outs.

Always, *always, always*, check that tenants have requested their final meter readings, and that the relevant utilities have an accurate forwarding address, by telephoning direct before you release deposit funds. And don't let suppliers try fobbing you off with data protection malarkey. Some utility companies can be downright awkward about this – but they soon come round if you tell them that you have a forwarding address and you'll share it. Again, I see little here that the Tenancy Deposit Scheme will change.

Don't let problems like these grind you down
It reads a great deal harder than the reality of a few phone calls and an inventory check-out to keep on top of management issues like this. Your building is a valuable piece of kit – the last thing you need is a blacklisted address through no fault of your own because of a tenant's bad debts. Or one that's allowed to slowly deteriorate because you didn't insist on maintaining the standards you first set.

Where to send unpaid bills
If your tenant moves on without leaving any forwarding address, return mail to the sender. Return bills to the sender with a copy of the lease and a signed letter stating the tenant's leaving date. Send back mail of unknown origin by scribbling 'no longer at this address' on the envelope and shoving them into the nearest mailbox. Do *not*

leave mail from old tenants hanging around in communal hallways: it's a godsend to fraudsters.

Under the existing system

Under the existing system, if your tenant doesn't agree your charges are reasonable you'll have to plough on, make your deductions and hope that any court challenges go your way. Whatever system is operating, courts (and any new arbitrator) are going to want evidence of damage/disrepair. Good practice produces evidence and should not be a problem for organised landlords.

Under the new Tenancy Deposit Schemes, notify your chosen Scheme provider that you are in dispute with your former tenant over damage costs and immediately transfer any disputed funds to your Scheme (read Part 2 for more details). If you still hold any *undisputed* balance, return it promptly to your former tenant within a maximum of ten days. Use cheques – they create proof of return. If you do decide to provide cash, ensure that your tenant gives you a receipt for any funds.

Does this kind of approach with tenants and deposits really work?
More often than not (though to be absolutely honest, most tenants need a minimal charge for a couple of hours' proper cleaning. It isn't a landlord's job to clear up after *anyone* for free.) But problems needing a whole new law haven't been caused by deduction of modest cleaning costs. It's been caused by the wholesale rifling of tenants hard earned money. The old system is a mess. Frankly, we should all hope the new one works better.

What tenants do now to protect themselves
With tens of million of pounds per year illegally deducted, some tenants have stopped listening to anyone. The deposit/inventory system exists to encourage tenants into a good standard of returns. Abuse has turned the system on its head. Many tenants now routinely withhold the final month's rent (meaning there's no deposit at all in reality). Hopefully this should change with the new Tenancy Deposit Scheme.

Who some real losers might be under these new Schemes

Perversely, as a colleague pointed out recently, the biggest losers here may well be tenants themselves. Many of us have found ways to speed up deposit refunds when good tenants have returned units in the expected condition. But tenants, especially ones who are now themselves obliged to use a third party if they don't agree over deduction costs, or whose landlords chooses to use the fully Custodial Scheme, may find the gap between leaving a property and receiving their deposit balances from the Tenancy Deposit Scheme significantly longer. We shall see.

How much deposit to charge

Landlords normally charge a four-week deposit: agents typically six weeks. For cheaper units, four weeks' deposit (plus four weeks' advance rent) is easier for many tenants to find than six – which widens your applicant pool. Stick to between four and six weeks – but never try hiking deposits beyond six weeks – you could end up in a legal mess over premiums, which give tenants more rights than a standard assured shorthold tenancy.

When to charge it

Usually on the day when tenants accept keys and sign leases. Varying this arrangement is fairly pointless but you can if you wish. (However, don't be too hasty. The new system requires the arrangements to be made to safeguard a tenant deposit within 14 days of receipt – not 14 days into the tenancy.)

And finally (under either system)

Ask every tenant with whom you've enjoyed a good relationship and to whom you're able to provide a full deposit refund if they'll need a reference. Then ask them for a written reference about you in return – as a landlord. Believe me, a few reassuring words from former tenants are worth more than any paltry few pound's worth of illegal deposit deductions to landlords wanting to do well.

— CHECKLIST/SUMMARY FOR PART 1 —

■ Make sure you charge between four and six weeks' rent as a maximum – two months' rent can create a legal premium.

- Make sure your tenant knows exactly how to get their deposit back – then always be as good as your word.

- Never agree to refund deposits as (or before) tenants move out. You'll need an empty unit and peace and quiet to go through a unit properly.

- Don't charge for wear and tear. A tenant has already paid for that with their rent.

- Don't try making unreasonable or inflated charges.

- In cases of major damage – you must get a witness, take photos and, where necessary, obtain estimates before even beginning the clear up. Keep your tenant fully informed as to why there's a hold up with the deposit return. In cases of disagreement over costs, where Schemes have been involved, notify the Scheme provider and send them the disputed sum of money in question.

- In cases of minor damage/cleaning, get on the phone and talk to your tenant before they start hollering about seeing you in court/ calling in arbitrators.

- Always obtain estimates for damage even if you intend rectifying it yourself, no court/arbitrator expects you to redecorate for love.

- Tenancy Application Forms should contain a statement explaining your system of always returning deposits in the form of a cheque to the tenant's next address. Stick with this as it has other benefits.

- Any tenant obtaining a full deposit refund is a perfect candidate to obtain and provide each-way references.

- Keep all receipts to do with any tenancy for a minimum of two years.

- Always take meter readings and check that tenants have arranged to pay their own closing accounts for the utilities before releasing funds you still hold.

- Make sure that you notify the local council/water company that your tenants no longer live there – and check their payments are up to date.

- Read the whole of this Lesson – deposits are important and about to change.

Part 2: The new Tenancy Deposit Scheme requirements

Having ploughed your way through Part 1 (and indeed the rest of this guide), you'll see that each element has an impact on everything else. Deposits, inventories, tenant selection and relationships are all part of the rich tapestry that make letting property such an interesting thing to do. So, simply safeguarding tenants' deposits will be no hardship for well informed, reasonable landlords. The people who'll struggle with this new legal requirement are landlords/agents who've grown used to making unreasonable profits from tenancy deposits. However, there are distinct landlord advantages to this new legislation that are being underplayed. Too many tenants have challenged the most reasonable charges by landlords on some pretty shoddy standards of return and damaged property. This new system should start levelling the playing field for both landlords and tenants. That has to be good news, but please don't expect such a massive legal upheaval to glide into place without teething troubles.

So, deposit legislation will affect *any deposit taken on any assured shorthold tenancy* established after 6 April 2007.

The following is brief because you have already read about reasonable behaviour and its importance in Part 1. There seems little point in someone else simply replicating the Q&A that the government's own website adequately covers. Check the original – it answers pretty much all you need to know about what is a relatively simple concept – see: *www.communities.gov.uk/tenancy.deposits*.

However, I am concerned by the absolute assumption by legislators that every landlord is comfortable using the internet. I suspect that this may cause some landlords problems so, if you are in any way confused, visit your local Citizens Advice Bureau – or your local authority's private rental department. Eventually, I hope that the publication arm of the government will produce another of its user-friendly booklets. Until then, if the internet is not your thing, you can contact the legislators themselves in writing at:

The Tenancy Deposit Protection Team
Housing Markets Division
Communities and Local Government
Zone 2/J 10
Eland House
Bressenden Place
London SW1 5DM
Tel: 020 7944 4400
Email: *tenancy.deposit@communities.gsi.gov.uk*

Here are some useful websites and phone numbers. The residential landlords excellent advisory site on: *www.rla.org.uk* has a good Q&A session on this topic that I can't improve on. Another useful contact point is The Dispute Service, tel: 0845 2267837 or email them at *deposits@tds.gb.com*. Other websites given in earlier lessons may also add to your knowledge. Alternatively, just Google 'Tenancy Deposit Scheme' and you will be overwhelmed. All landlords need to get to grips with what has become a mountain of information, which is currently in a changeable state and is likely to remain so for a while, considering the scale of the changes due.

This guide can only realistically provide a taster – more would require a dedicated guide. For snapshot information, use a combination of pointers here and some of the websites. Not surprisingly, the information system is currently in a state of considerable flux as Schemes gear up to take on national projects. Expect teething problems but eventually glitches should get ironed out and we could well be left with a far better system.

An overview

All landlords and agents have to start using this system so familiarise yourself with your options and choose one for all future deposits.

This new Tenancy Deposit Scheme has *two* choices of Scheme *type*. You need to decide which type you prefer as that choice remains with the landlord/agent.

Scheme type one

This is a fully custodial scheme where the company (Scheme) holds the whole deposit for the entire tenancy. This option has only one national provider:

The Deposit Protection Service (the DPS)
Website: *www.depositprotection.com*
Tel: 0870 707 1707

This company is part of a bigger company called Computershare Services Investor plc. There are no charges to either landlord or tenant for using this scheme. Instead, its costs will be covered by the interest generated by holding deposit monies on reserve which, as these schemes gather momentum, will become an eye-watering sum of money.

Note: I will be very interested indeed to see figures released on just how much interest generated will be eaten up by the costs of administering this Scheme. As yet, the government's being a wee bit coy about releasing the operating figures.

Scheme type two

These are insurance-backed schemes. This, in essence, means that by taking fees and charges from landlords/agents, these Schemes will be able to insure deposits, thus protecting tenants from rogue landlords/agents who fail to return/routinely overcharge against deposits.

Put simply, where rogue landlords refuse to repay all or part of a tenant's deposits, the Scheme will repay the tenant. Then, that Scheme will chase debtor landlords. In this way, tenants won't have to go to court to recover their money because it will be insured.

Note: Now you see why such stringent sanctions have been introduced to force all landlords to comply, because these systems can only work if all landlords are registered.

There are currently two insurance-backed Schemes available with more in the pipeline. If landlords get an increased supply of service providers this should help improve competitiveness in their pricing. So far, you can choose either:

Tenancy Deposit Solutions Ltd (TDSL)
Website: *www.mydeposits.co.uk*

or

The Tenancy Deposit Scheme (TDS)
Website: *www.tds.gb.com*
Tel: 0845 226 7837

And now for a little more detail on how they should work. For a fuller picture all landlords must research carefully using the resources provided earlier in Part 2.

Option 1: The custodial option

The custodial scheme is simple to understand. Landlords/agents pass over the entire deposit and receive legally required documentation for themselves and tenants in return. This must be done within 14 days of accepting any deposit. The whole deposit remains with the custodial scheme until the end of the tenancy. Then, so long as property is returned in good order, once notified, the Scheme will reimburse the tenant direct within ten days.

If, however, deductions are required for damage, one of two things happens:

1. Landlord and tenant agree a deduction and notify the DPS, who will apportion monies accordingly – again within ten days.

2. Landlord and tenant cannot agree how much deductions should be, and notify the DPS that they are in dispute over costs.

Disagreements (or disputes) trigger yet more options. In cases of dispute, the Scheme will hold onto that proportion of the deposit that is in dispute. The undisputed balance should be refunded direct to the tenant. Beyond that, several things can happen:

1. Landlord and tenant both agree to use something called the Alternative Dispute Resolution Service (ADR), which will be binding and therefore parties lose their court option. ADR systems of arbitration are free to both landlord and tenant. This Scheme's arbitration will be backed by the Chartered Institute of Arbitrators, whose expertise will be used to resolve disputes and apportion monies.

2. Both parties may prefer to go direct to court (a small word of warning here – courts may well take a dim view of claimants clogging up their system when a perfectly good ADR was available).

3. War breaks out and neither party can agree a thing, let alone which system to use to resolve disputes – where the suggestion (at this stage) appears to be that ADR will then start.

4. Or, one party can't even contact the other – in which case a single party can instigate a claim for either partial or full reimbursement via ADR.

Option 2: Insurance-based Schemes

The second option for landlords to consider is the insurance-backed Schemes of which there are currently two providers – but expect more soon. Unlike its cousin the custodial Scheme, there will be some fees for landlords. This provision will also offer an ADR, which will be free to both landlord and tenant as an alternative to using the courts.

Despite some up-front costs, I expect this option to be popular for a number of reasons, simply because in many ways, many landlords will find it has a much more familiar feel to it. Using this Scheme, landlords still take deposits from tenants, still hold onto them and still return them direct to tenants – *unless any dispute arises over deposit deductions*.

What landlords wanting to use these Schemes *must* do is choose a supplier (provided earlier) and contact them to register. Then, when deposits are accepted, landlords must *immediately notify* their service, then pay an insurance premium to safeguard that specific deposit. Your chosen Scheme will provide the correct legal paperwork to both landlord and tenant. And again, this deposit must be notified to your Scheme within 14 days of receipt.

In all cases of disputes over deposit deductions, landlords must immediately notify their Scheme. Any disputed amount of the deposit must then be immediately handed over by the landlord to that Scheme, which will hold onto all disputed funds until resolution. Then, using similar processes to the ones briefly outlined under custodial arrangements, matters over disputed funds will be managed between landlords, tenants and the Scheme's resolution processes, or indeed the courts. The undisputed deposit balance still held by landlords (if any) should be returned to tenants, again, within ten days. The Scheme will be responsible for dispersing the disputed funds according to the dispute procedure or court decisions.

All landlords are advised to keep a very careful eye on these matters. Not knowing what you were supposed to do will be *no* defence if you breach this new legislation.

Now, I'm sure you have many more questions so, for specifics, start surfing. I can only advise you how to try steering clear of too much trouble in the first place and outline the Scheme options here. However, I have some questions of my own that I'm sure that many of you will share:

- Who regulates these private companies?
- What is a landlord sanction and a tenant sanction, when things go wrong?
- What happens when forms don't arrive?
- What happens when funds don't get transferred on time?
- Who will be training all these new arbitrators?
- Will *all* arbitrators receive genuine training or will private companies with an eye on their bottom line be allowed to use less well qualified staff than, say, chartered arbitrators?
- Who will be monitoring the quality of deduction assessments?

■ Are there consequences for poor decisions?

■ What happens if the costs of these Schemes begins skyrocketing?

And on, and on, and on!

There has also been a huge information disparity in introducing this legislation.

How are the tens of thousands of independent private landlords who don't belong to organisations being reached – despite government claims of an advertising campaign? How on earth are *tenants* to learn of all these new rights? How can they enforce them without losing tenure on a six month lease? Who is expected to report landlords who continue to hold deposits? Will tenants believe that the benefits of challenging their awkward landlord about deposit protection will outweigh their genuine fear of losing their home? Or is the introduction of this, like so much landlord/tenant regulation, a rule for the compliant majority, which the rogue landlords will continually flout...again! And on and on...

Then one final depressing thought. I am becoming seriously concerned about just how many more third parties can tap merrily into letting's revenue. What used to be a simple transaction between two parties is now remorselessly supporting a huge range of commercial interests with ever-open beaks. Over the past decade, tenants have had a huge range of costs built into their rent. First it was soaring prices caused by interest charges on borrowings. Then management charges (to say nothing of the additional costs to tenants whose landlords use agents, before, during, and after their tenancies). To this endless list, we can now add some lost interest payments to fund an entire nationwide scheme. Okay, interest may not be a great loss – but it was the straw that broke the camel's back, not the bag of bricks!

Let's not forget that every single penny generated, earned and spent by our industry comes originally from our tenants' pockets. These escalating costs combined with virtually no security of tenure may eventually start impacting on tenant demand. Tenant resources are already stretched almost to breaking point in many cases without increasing their costs, concerns or responsibilities further. As a wise

French economist once said (about taxation) the secret is to pluck as many feathers from the goose with the minimum of hissing. We might all do well to remember that soon our tenants may begin hissing a little too loudly for comfort – if we don't begin to recognise some of their genuine financial realities.

Whys and wherefores

In principle, I like the idea of a better system. Both landlords and tenants sometimes struggle to be dispassionate. The landlord/agent may indeed be trying to make unfair charges. On the other hand, most tenants have absolutely no idea how much things cost to repair – let alone replace. Put that realistic figure on paper and tenants often *see* theft – when in many cases, it is simply that workmen don't come cheap – especially in the south-east, where builders walking through the door costs in excess of £100 a day.

Look at websites and start checking out service providers. Suckers for punishment might try looking up even more housing proposals about to hit the rental sector called 'Renting Homes' under the Law Commission's 'Review of Tenure' proposals. Information can be accessed on progress of the Scheme from: *www.tds.gb.com*, from the Citizens Advice Bureau or from any small (or residential) landlords associations.

— CHECKLIST/SUMMARY PART 2 —

▪ Keep your sense of proportion. This is necessary legislation because bad practitioners have ruined an excellent system.

▪ There will be two main scheme types – custodial and insurance-based.

▪ All deposits accepted after April 2007 must be registered with one Scheme or another. They cannot legally be held independently.

▪ Landlords trying to ignore these rules face huge financial penalties plus a loss of possession rights. This law means business.

- Face facts – until the law changed, far too many tenants refused to pay the final month's rent – that unpalatable reality meant that landlords didn't hold meaningful deposits.

- This new system should clarify matters. Landlord and agent abuse should be stopped in its tracks.

- Tenants usually have less money than landlords – they're the ones who face serious difficulties if this new legislation holds up their deposit repayments.

- Tenants will also need to be sensible under this new system or risk tying up large chunks of deposit for weeks at a time.

- The trickier rules apply to *disputed* tenancy deposit returns. Hone your people skills and learn how to avoid most disputes.

- Behave fairly. That was what you should always have been doing – if not – well *now* is an excellent time to turn over a new leaf.

- It's going to be a hard job indeed to decide what costs to insist on and which to waive simply because of the trouble and bureaucracy.

- Yet again, the only people making money out of these schemes are third parties.

Read the whole of this lesson, the checklist isn't adequate.

Lesson 11

Ending tenancies

What usually happens at the end of tenancies?

Forget scaremongers. The overwhelming majority of tenancies wind themselves up without any legal issues whatsoever. Let property is temporary housing for tenants. Most landlords are letting out property over many years that far outlast a tenant's wish to stay.

Nevertheless, let's be realistic. If novice landlords worry about leases, they positively fret about how they'll shut down an unsatisfactory tenancy. They needn't. So long as landlords stay inside the safe confines of an assured shorthold lease, they've genuinely nothing to fear about ending troublesome tenancies. And, if that wasn't peace of mind enough, the whole basis in law of an assured shorthold is that landlords have a legal right to close down any tenancy they choose, *for no reason whatsoever*, once that initial fixed term has expired – in other words, if you've followed my earlier advice, after six short months.

Notice only grounds for possession under Section 21

This is the pearl in the proverbial shorthold oyster. Section 21 of the Housing Act 1988 gives landlords with assured shorthold leases absolute freedom to choose whether or not to continue any tenancy once its initial fixed term expires. Which is why landlords should insist on testing out new tenants with a six month start, throughout which you're entitled to your rent – at the end of which you can end the tenancy relatively easily, using the courts of course. Read on.

Once the landlord receives a notice letter from their tenant

The *overwhelming majority* of tenancies don't end with courts. Tenancies usually conclude when the tenant wants to move. What will usually happen is that your tenant will notify you that they plan to leave the

159

property on a certain date (request verbal notice in writing to cover your back). Tenancies are formal and always need paperwork, which must be stored.

This written notice will usually trigger a few matters.

1. Initially, landlords should contact outgoing tenants and ask if they still have their copy of the inventory, schedules, etc to help them return the property as found. If not, pop photocopies in the post to tenants to avoid amnesia.

2. It should also trigger a letter of confirmation from the landlord, along with a written explanation that you intend to exercise your right to show prospective tenants the property during the last 28 days and some tentative suggestions on timing.

3. Don't overpower your existing tenant – remember that they are still paying rent and it's terribly invasive having strangers walk round your bedroom at the best of times, so be considerate.

If your tenant wants to move out before their initial fixed term expires

Sometimes, a tenant wants or needs to move before their initial fixed term has expired. This will necessitate landlords having a far firmer dialogue. Tenants have rights – they also have responsibilities – one of them is that they remain liable for the rent for the entire fixed term. Of course, this isn't open to abuse. When tenants find themselves moving for reasons beyond their control (eg a hurried job deployment) landlords should explain to the tenants their responsibilities, then try to find an amicable settlement. And though the law in this respect is equitable between landlord and tenant, landlords who rest on their laurels entirely – hoping to bill a long gone tenant for three or four months without lifting a finger to re-let – might find themselves challenged in court. Landlords are expected to make *reasonable* attempts to find a suitable replacement and will need proof of advertising and viewings. Waiting it out in the luxurious position of having all the benefits (rent) and none of the liabilities (a tenant) will not be deemed fair by a court.

Finding a new tenant

The businesslike thing to do here is to begin re-advertising to find a new tenant. Once you have found a suitable alternative, the liabilities of the first tenant are obviously discharged. You'll find that tenants who are forced to move on quickly and with all the rental liabilities that incurs, are the most helpful you'll ever encounter in terms of tidying up before viewings.

If you can't genuinely find a replacement (though heaven only knows why if you found one before), then you'll need to bill your tenant for rent unpaid throughout the contract. Don't hold your breath waiting for the cheques. Tenants can be veritable will-o'-the-wisps once they've moved.

Landlords letting out their own home on a short-term basis

Up and down the country, there are potential landlords who, usually for work-related reasons, decide that letting out their own home is a better option than selling up. These landlords still need to stay within the comfortable breadth of the assured shorthold protocol. In other words, don't try letting for periods of less than six months, because that fixed term offers you the maximum benefits. However, life has a nasty habit of not always conforming to our plans. Anyone who wants to let out their own home on a reasonably temporary basis might feel happier to serve what's known as a 'prior notice' ground on their tenant (a simple letter explaining that the property is your main home, let out temporarily and quoting the appropriate ground in full – read on) before exchanging leases. This establishes *a mandatory* ground for possession – or in plain language – it establishes an additional (indisputable) legal reason for the courts to grant you possession. Keep the initial fixed term to six months. Beyond that, any landlord can apply to the courts for possession for no reason whatsoever.

Landlords with mortgages

Landlords who have borrowings against the property they intend to let out (especially Buy to Let landlords) will probably be advised by their lender that a different 'prior notice' ground *must* be served. This applies to anyone with a mortgage and landlords would be breaching their covenant with their lender if they omitted to notify their tenants, in writing, that the property is subject to a mortgage, which was granted before the tenancy. Should the lender want (or need) to sell the property (usually to cover mortgage arrears), this ground allows possession at any time through the courts. This particular 'ground for possession' is one of the few that can be initiated before the fixed term has expired.

When tenancies start to go wrong, what should I do?

Hold your breath and count to ten before doing a thing. Starting legal processes against your tenants is the final nail in the relationship coffin. Avoid court as anything but the *last resort*. Misunderstandings, over-bearing landlords and late payers are two a penny. What this industry is often a bit short of is common sense – and landlords can be as deaf as any tenants.

Managing well minimises problems. Make your tenants aware of their responsibilities and try to work things out long before things get to court. Agents can afford court delays – you *can't*.

Finding solutions is usually better than using courts

The route to solutions is, more often than not, a negotiation. Independents enjoy a level of flexibility that an agent can only dream about. You can make choices for yourself, ease pressure points, look for lateral solutions that an agent wouldn't dare suggest to an angry landlord. Tenants can get in a terrible jam sometimes. Often they've been silly. Sometimes, circumstances have genuinely left them in a dilemma. *Talk* to them. If rent is the problem, try any solution to limp things along until the end of your fixed term. Offering a fall-back position (agreeing to let tenants pay a bit more each week to get their rent back in line for example) is often much cheaper in the medium term than going to court ever is. For tenants whose initial fixed term has expired, initiate possession proceedings by all means, but try limping things along with reasonable dialogue or risk losing all future payments – the giving of formal notice followed by court process (including bailiffs) usually takes three to four months. That's a big hole in your annual accounts that might be avoidable if you can bite your tongue.

If you've no alternative but to use the courts

Once legal proceedings are initiated, all hope of discussion and compromise flies out of the window. Goodwill evaporates. Rent stops right there and then – I can almost guarantee it. Getting possession takes time – and it *must* be done legally at every stage. This is a hands-off process for landlords. It's a form-filling, fee-paying, loss-making, frustrating waiting game. Even once you have a possession order you can't act if the tenant fails to leave on the date the court sets for them to go. You must fill out another form, write another cheque and arrange for court-appointed bailiffs to evict. Doing anything else is the route to massive fines for illegal eviction. UK law is very clear. Courts and their officers evict tenants. Anyone else doing so is committing a major criminal offence.

Something you probably don't know

Tenants in a jam (say those who lose their job) are in a Catch 22 position when courts set a date for them to leave (a possession order in favour of the landlord). Believe it or not, leaving *voluntarily* on that date – without being actually evicted by bailiffs – is regarded by most local housing departments as making yourself *deliberately homeless*. Therefore, all tenants in this position are advised by the Citizens Advice Bureau to stay put until the bailiffs arrive. Sometimes what can look like bloody mindedness is simply a tenant doing the best they can to avoid sleeping on the streets.

Making the best of a bad tenancy by using notice only grounds

The rule of thumb is that, wherever possible, ride out the initial fixed term. Doing so enables you to use your notice only grounds (Section 21 of the Housing Act 1988). In other words, the tenancy is up and you want your property back. This is a fail-safe mechanism, guaranteed to obtain possession from any court as it isn't optional.

What do I have to do to give a Section 21 notice?

Simply write to your tenant giving them a minimum of *two months' notice before* the end of their fixed term (or at any time after this has expired) and confirm that you'll want your property back by the end of the fixed term date on the lease (or alternate later date). Beyond the initial fixed term you're still required to give two months' written notice. Wherever possible, don't antagonise tenants, this is a delicate process. Angry tenants tend not to behave well. Make sure you send this letter well in advance — and a follow-up reminder is a good idea — all to arrive more than two months before their fixed term expires. Always use recorded delivery and keep copies of correspondence and receipts to show date of posting.

Follow the simple rules

1. There's no special form for this. All you're legally required to do is to write to your tenants (keep a copy and make sure that you can prove receipt by the tenant by recording the delivery or by hand delivering the letter with a witness).

2. You must give at least *two months'* written notice that you require possession.

3. You must ask them to leave on a date *after* the fixed term ends.

4. If your tenancy has run on beyond that initial fixed term and become a statutory periodic, the date for leaving must be the last day of a tenancy period (the last day before a rent payment is due).

5. The letter *must* state that you require possession under Section 21 of the Housing Act 1988.

6. Add your name and address, the address of the property concerned, the date their tenancy began and the date that the initial fixed term expires(ed).

7. It's a good idea to send a photocopy of the original lease (but hold on to the original — you may need to provide this to the court).

Note: for tenancies that started *before* 28 February 1997 special rules may apply here and you need to take specialist advice on the best way to obtain possession.

When things go wrong at an early stage

Of course, tenancies don't always go well. Sometimes landlords and/or tenants allow the relationship to deteriorate. At other times, even the most responsible landlord can find themselves housing a tenant who will not pay rent – or will pay very erratically. Tenants might be bothering the neighbours, or damaging your property. They could even be dealing drugs or running a car workshop in the yard. They may have moved in friends against your clear instructions and the lease. In these circumstances, you clearly can't limp a tenancy along. You will then have to act – using the courts at a much earlier date.

How difficult is it to get a possession order during the initial fixed term?

It's certainly not easy. Tenants only enjoy security of tenure for such a short time (during these first fixed terms) that courts take closing one down very seriously. In these circumstances, you've no alternative but to use one or more of the 17 grounds for possession that the Housing Act 1988 provides for this purpose.

The Housing Act 1988 provides 17 legitimate legal reasons for a court to grant possession to a landlord – a few even during the fixed term. There are two types of grounds – mandatory and discretionary.

During the initial fixed term, landlords have to *prove* to a court that problems do genuinely exist. This is a treacherous area for landlords, who need to be able *to substantiate and prove their case in court*. To do this, they have to decide which legal reason(s) they will be seeking to prove.

During the fixed term you can only seek possession if one of the grounds 2, 8, 10, 14, 15 or 17 apply, the terms of the tenancy make provision for it to be ended on any of these grounds and you can prove your case in court.

At the end of the fixed term, you can seek possession on any of these grounds that apply. And, when tenants become problematic, it may be better to use one of the faster to obtain grounds than using the Section 21 route, which requires two months' written notice, where some of these additional legal grounds require a much shorter period of notice. However, anything other than a Section 21 requires *special forms* to be used (available from Oyez and other suppliers).

These special forms are called 'Notice seeking possession of property let on an assured tenancy or an assured agricultural tenancy'. These must be completed by the landlord/agent and delivered to the tenant. Always take a photocopy. Make sure that you can prove your tenant received this notice by delivering by hand with a witness or sending the document by recorded delivery.

When filling in these forms, it's important to write out the legal ground(s) that you are using *exactly* as it appears in the legislation (as below or in your handy landlord booklet from the Department of Communities and Local Government).

Mandatory grounds

Mandatory grounds – ones that if proven the court must grant possession to the landlord. If proved, courts will grant an absolute possession order to the landlord.

Discretionary grounds

Grounds where the court may, or may not, agree to give a possession order.

These are more numerous, but even if you prove your case, the court may decide NOT to grant *full possession* (which is why so many of us limp things along until we are certain that we have section 21 rights). They may grant a suspended possession order – in other words, give your tenant a last chance.

It remains, during that fixed term, a costly game of chance – a frustrating and pricey business for landlords chasing erratic rent, whose tenant suddenly stumps up a couple of weeks rent on the court steps – promptly burying your ground.

List of all grounds available to landlords

Mandatory grounds

(Note: prior notice grounds mentioned below are ones that must be incorporated into the contract that the tenant signs – either written into a gap provided on an off-the-peg lease, or incorporated into a tailor-made one.)

- **Ground 1 prior notice ground**

  You used to live in the property as your only or main home. Or, so long as you or someone before you did not buy the property after the tenancy started, you or your spouse require it to live in as your main home.

- **Ground 2 prior notice ground**

  The property is subject to a mortgage which was granted before the tenancy started and the lender, usually a bank or building society, wants to sell it, normally to pay off mortgage arrears.

- **Ground 3 prior notice ground**

  The tenancy is for a fixed term of not more than eight months and at some time during the 12 months before the tenancy started, the property was let for a holiday.

- **Ground 4 prior notice ground**

  The tenancy is for a fixed term of not more than 12 months and at some time during the 12 months before the tenancy started, the property was let to students by an educational establishment such as a university or college.

- **Ground 5 prior notice ground**

  The property is held for use for a minister of religion and is now needed for that purpose.

- **Ground 6**

  You intend to substantially redevelop the property and cannot do so with the tenant there. This ground cannot be used where you, or someone before you, bought the property with an existing tenant, or where work could be carried out without the tenant having to move. The tenant's removal expenses will have to be paid.

■ **Ground 7**

The former tenant, who must have had a contractual periodic tenancy or statutory periodic tenancy, has died in the 12 months before possession proceedings started and there is no one living there who has a right to succeed to the tenancy.

■ **Ground 8**

The tenant owed at least two months' rent if the tenancy is on a monthly basis or eight weeks' rent if it is on a weekly basis, both when you gave notice seeking possession and at the date of the court hearing.

Discretionary grounds

(Where the court may or may not decide to grant possession to the landlord.)

■ **Ground 9**

Suitable alternative accommodation is available for the tenant, or will be when the court order takes effect. The tenant's removal expenses will have to be paid.

■ **Ground 10**

The tenant was behind with his or her rent when you served notice seeking possession and when you began court proceedings.

■ **Ground 11**

Even if the tenant was not behind with his or her rent when you started proceedings, he or she has been persistently late in paying rent.

■ **Ground 12**

The tenant has broken one or more of the terms of the tenancy agreement, except the obligation to pay rent.

■ **Ground 13**

The condition of the property has got worse because of the behaviour of the tenant or any other person living there.

■ **Ground 14**

The tenant, or someone living or visiting the property has caused or is likely to cause a nuisance or annoyance to someone living in the locality; or has been convicted of using the property; or allowing it to be used for immoral or illegal purposes; or an arrestable offence committed in the property or the locality.

■ **Ground 15**

The condition of the furniture in the property has got worse because it has been ill-treated by the tenant or any other person living there.

■ **Ground 16**

The tenancy was granted because the tenant was employed by you, or a former landlord, but he or she is no longer employed by you.

■ **Ground 17**

You were persuaded to grant the tenancy on the basis of a false statement knowingly or recklessly made by the tenant, or a person acting at the tenant's instigation. (Remember your handy signed tenancy application procedure.)

Notice you must give the tenant before using grounds for possession

Each of these grounds has a particular notice period, which must expire *before* the landlord can apply to the court.

For grounds 3, 4, 8, 10, 11, 12, 13, 15 or 17 – at least *two weeks'* written notice must be given.

For grounds 1, 2, 5, 6, 7, 9 and 16 – at least *two months'* written notice must be given.

For ground 14 – this is the only ground where possession may be sought immediately after notifying your tenant in writing on the special form mentioned earlier.

What are my realistic options?

Put simply, you've two broad alternatives if you want your property back.

■ If things are not brilliant, but bearable (say the rent's sometimes a bit slow or the place is beginning to look a bit care worn), the best advice is to try to stick out the tenancy for the first six months (that initial fixed term). Two months before the end of the fixed term, write to your tenant explaining that you'll be exercising your rights under Section 21 of the Housing Act 1988 and that you'll want the property back at the end of the fixed term. Waiting until the end of the fixed term makes sense wherever possible because, if they don't move out by that date, you can then use the *accelerated possession procedure* for a speedy resolution through the courts, and usually without even attending (more details below).

■ However, if your tenant is accruing significant arrears – or is obviously causing trouble or damage, you may need to act earlier to protect yourself. This requires a judgement by the courts gained only by evidence of significant breach of contract.

Do landlords need legal representation to end an assured shorthold lease?

No. It's simply not required under the 1988 Act. Nor do landlords have to work their way through the detailed 'clause 8 sub-section, para. iv, etc' that websites and glossy agent's blurb so often use to undermine an independent's confidence. It's fluff, designed to convince you that repossession is too complicated to be carried out by anyone but them. Tosh! All you need to terminate even the most contentious assured shorthold tenancy is a bit of practical common sense – the right forms and a few fees for service.

If I don't feel confident enough to go for possession myself, what else can I do?

Nervousness and the steady stream of court fees can take their toll – especially now, when so many landlords are part-timers who don't do this regularly. And even the most straightforward rules can seem complicated to those who don't feel familiar enough with them.

Two options

Option 1
Many landlords (and, I'm assured, many agents too) use a specialist service for this. It can give peace of mind to someone happy enough to do everything else but evict. The usual cost is around £399 – so my advice is don't pay over the odds for a straightforward service.

There are a few specialist services out there for those of you who want the confidence of a *guarantee of possession* for a set fee. See *www.landlordaction.co.uk* who do nothing but evict shorthold tenants for any number of reasons. They've carried out thousands over the last few years and their services are guaranteed to provide you with possession. Look online for other firms with proven track records.

Option 2

Alternatively, any high street solicitor will take a case through the courts and get you possession for a fee. It's likely to cost more than the possession services but high street solicitors are all small businesses and are open to fee negotiation, so get yourself a fixed-fee deal.

In summary, repossession can be obtained by a simple court process carried out by:

- any independent landlord using simple forms available from legal stationers and courts and completed in triplicate then returned to the courts with the appropriate fee;
- services which specialise in possession for assured shorthold leases;
- any high street solicitor.

Accelerated possession procedure

Those of you applying for possession at the end of a fixed term can use a special process called *accelerated possession*. They are speedy and cheap(ish), a little over £130 at time of writing. One drawback is that you can't charge your tenants any owed rent using this process – it's for possession only. It can only be used where a written tenancy (lease) exists.

County courts will send you an Accelerated Possession Procedure Form N5B. Follow the (simple) instructions and fill in the three copies required. Return all three copies to the court with your fee. They do the rest and let you know how things are proceeding.

So long as you can provide evidence of a lease with an expired fixed term and copy letters giving two months' notice, the court should expedite the possession very efficiently on your behalf (typically three to four weeks).

Although landlords can't use accelerated possession to recoup lost rent, most are more troubled by obtaining possession by this stage.

Lost rent

Alternatively (I told you, this legislation was comprehensive), if you do want to make a claim for lost rent too, you'll need to complete a different form from the county court. This process takes longer as evidence from both parties is needed. To make a comprehensive claim for possession plus lost income (and indeed damage) you'll need a Form N5 from your county court (again three copies must be filled in and cheques provided, then the court will progress matters).

If you want to claim possession and other costs you need to tick the 'forfeiture of the lease' box on the form and, if unpaid rent is also an issue, you'll tick the rent arrears box too (or whatever else is appropriate).

You'll need to write out the precise legal wording of the grounds that you are relying on in the appropriate box. Check the list I gave earlier and choose the most appropriate grounds. Again, follow the instructions, attach leases, written notices and any other supporting documentation.

On balance, if a large amount of rent is outstanding or considerable damage needs to be claimed for, landlords may be prepared to wait the extra few weeks (with extra rent loss).

When things go horribly wrong

However, there will be rare circumstances when issues are too problematic to wait around for fixed terms to expire. We're entering 'tenant from hell' territory – ugly – if fairly rare.

I'm acutely conscious that saying how rare such instances are doesn't console the landlord in the midst of such a tenancy. And tenants from hell do exist and many are seasoned practitioners of abuse. However tight our procedures, some lousy tenants can and do slip through all our nets.

Protected by that initial six months' security of tenure, some resolutely bad tenants can run up alarming debts and problems. Frustrating. Absolutely infuriating. And a nightmare to any landlord who has embarked on a letting without sufficient back-up funds to tide them over a very lean patch, which can sometimes drag on for months.

After the court has awarded you possession

Things are almost, but not quite, at an end. English courts don't evict people on the spot. Usually tenants will be given a date sometime soon by which they must have vacated the premises.

So, even with an absolute possession order, there will still be a small time-lag. After this date, if the tenant still hasn't moved on, you'll need to contact the court again. Fill out the form requesting the court bailiff to enforce the possession order, pay another fee and wait for a few more days. The bailiff will notify both you and your tenants of his/her impending arrival. It is the job of the court bailiff service *not the landlord* – to evict tenants.

Under English law, illegally evicting a tenant remains a very serious offence, and incurs hefty fines.

Whys and wherefores

Excellent information is available on possession matters at *www.communities.gov.uk* in the online section for private landlords. The website *www.rics.co.uk* has a very handy section, as does *www.rla.org.uk*, which also has a handy Q&A section. The site *www.landlordaction.co.uk* has a dedicated telephone helpline to advise landlords who've run into problems. Alternatively, landlords can carry out all legal processes online at *www.courtservice.gov.uk*.

Beyond that, as usual, the practicalities of how to turn round the problem tenancies don't seem to be anywhere but here. However, any landlord who is running up against problems would do well to consider contacting their Citizens Advice Bureau – landlords are citizens too. Or, if you're really unsure about whether or not you have reasonable grounds to apply for possession within the fixed term – a half-hour consultation with a local solicitor may help to clarify things.

— CHECKLIST/SUMMARY —

■ Most tenancies end naturally – using the law is rare in well managed units.

■ If your tenant gives one month's written notice of their intention to leave, use that time wisely to get hold of your next tenant.

■ When tenants try to leave before their initial fixed term has expired, discuss the implications with them. If they still need to move, try to get another tenant in place to release them from their contractual liabilities – or risk having to explain why you didn't.

■ Bite your tongue before threatening tenants with possession. Court is the worst option for landlords – a last, not a first resort.

■ Limp deteriorating tenancies along wherever possible to the end of fixed terms.

■ Any landlord can – after the fixed term has expired – obtain possession using the Section 21 route – which is guaranteed.

■ Using accelerated possession after the fixed term has ended is a quicker route to possession, but doesn't allow a landlord to recoup lost rent.

■ Usual court processes take a bit longer – but do allow landlords to claim unpaid rent.

■ Landlords with very bad tenants *mustn't* be afraid of trying for possession on good, provable grounds, during the fixed term.

■ If you go down this route, you will need evidence that satisfies the judge before he will grant you a possession order. Keep rent records. Get photographs of damage. If the police have been involved, get something in writing from them. Do whatever you can to make sure the court can see that this is not a frivolous application.

Lesson 12

The *serious* responsibilities

Taking your responsibilities seriously isn't a matter of luck. It's down to knowledge and application. Although this lesson is vital, it's also one that requires little explanation, making it relatively short. Ignore any of these rules at your peril.

The letting rules

In any form of business, there are rules that govern safety. You don't expect a trip to Tesco to result in death or injury – and tenants shouldn't have to dice with death to live in your property either. Check all or any in particular with Trading Standards.

Not following the rules can invalidate your insurance cover

Something vital that many reckless landlords forget is that their own insurance is likely to be void if they don't ensure that the property has been let in full compliance within the law. Keeping abreast of the new Housing in Multiple Occupation rules is now a *must* for every modern landlord.

The principles of safety

Landlords are responsible for safety. Where specific rules haven't been drawn up, common law protects tenants from injury or negligence caused by actions (or their lack) by landlords.

Insurance

A routine building and contents policy with public liability cover is *not* sufficient for private landlords. Landlords really should contact an independent insurance broker. Modern landlords should always protect themselves by purchasing 'property owner's liability insurance'. Without it, an individual landlord may find themselves *personally liable* for any claims against them. Not a good place to be.

Being insured isn't an excuse to forget about routine safety either. Certainly, insurance will cover a landlord's accidents. But not, say, if no effort is made to tack down a dangerous stair carpet. It may cover slipping on wet leaves – but not if they fell three months ago. Getting rent means accepting responsibility. Landlords forget that simple equation at their financial peril.

To furnish or not

More and more landlords are being advised to offer 'part furnished' property in order to offset the furniture liabilities. But markets always win and very few tenants own furniture. Furnish properly (which doesn't mean expensively) and you'll have peace of mind.

Be careful how you interpret 'furnished'. 'Furnished' has the basics 'bed, carpets, sofas, curtains, fridges, table and chairs, cooker, etc'. Keep it simple. Keep it safe.

Don't over-provide. It's unnecessary to provide irons/boards, kettles, cutlery, televisions, bedding, etc. Indeed the more you provide, the more cluttered the contract and the greater your own liabilities, increasing both management time and responsibilities.

Look at your unit dispassionately. Will half a dozen knives and forks really clinch a deal or put up the rent? If not – leave them out. Provide enough basic furniture that enables tenants to live in comfort, provide extras only where they're going to up the rent.

The more you provide – the wider your liability

That abused iron can become just as lethal as a faulty boiler – but much harder to remember and repair bills for superfluous items can exceed the values they ever added. Furnish safely – never unnecessarily.

All furniture in tenanted property must comply with the Furniture and Furnishings (Fire Safety) Regulations 1988, as announced.

The Regulations apply to:

■ Armchairs.

- Three-piece suites.

- Sofa beds, futons and other convertible items.

- Beds – bases and headboards, mattresses divans and pillows must all meet BS 117.

- All nursery furniture.

- Garden furniture where it may be used indoors.

- Fitted covers, stretch covers, cushions and seat pads.

Furniture which *does* comply carries an obvious manufacturer's label and this label must be permanent and non-detachable. This label assures the purchaser that upholstered items have fire-resistant filling, and have passed the prescribed 'match resistance' and 'cigarette' tests.

Items which are exempt from the Regulations are:

- Furniture manufactured before 1950.

- Bedding.

- Mattress covers.

- Curtains.

- Carpets.

The penalties for ignoring the law (which is rigorously enforced by Trading Standards departments) are:

- Six months' imprisonment.

- Potential manslaughter charges.

- A fine of £5,000.

- Civil damages claimed by tenants.

- Invalid insurance.

- A criminal record.

Gas safety

The Gas Safety (Installation and Use) Regulations 1998 affect every single landlord in the country and are very clear.

■ All gas appliance fitting and maintenance must be carried out by Corgi registered installers *and only by* Corgi registered installers.

■ All gas appliances provided by landlords must be certified safe by a Corgi registered gas engineer at least once every year.

■ Once inspected, the engineer will provide landlords with a certificate often referred to as a Gas Safety Certificate, which must be dated. *All* landlords are obliged to make sure that a valid certificate is available for all appliances and to make this available for their tenants.

■ Don't just assume that anyone who claims to be Corgi registered is. Always check the credentials of new tradespersons by calling The Corgi association, Tel: 01256 372 300.

The consequences of failing to comply with gas safety

Failure to comply with this basic safety requirement is a criminal offence. Regulation is enforced by the Health and Safety Executive who has extensive powers to fine or imprison landlords who flout this rule. And no wonder. This industry still experiences dozens of deaths every year to say nothing of the countless cases of brain damage associated with carbon monoxide poisoning. Where landlords use agents, it becomes the agent's liability to ensure certificates are kept up to date. Landlords *must* make certain that their agent is complying with this rule.

WARNING ANECDOTE

This story was provided by a hysterical parent who didn't know how to proceed against some outrageous behaviour. Her son's shared house had a problematic gas fire, with no Gas Safety Certificate and which the landlord and agency had shown little inclination to repair. Given the chilly weather, the cold students decided to call in the Gas Board to pay for the repair themselves.

But far from being willing to repair, the Gas Board's qualified engineer promptly condemned the gas fire, disconnected it and plastered a 'WARNING – DANGEROUS APPLIANCE' sticker over the knob. Time marched on and the tenants gave notice to leave in July, prompting the landlord to begin viewings for prospective new student intake. Arriving early, his preparations didn't include switching on lamps or worrying about the smell. Instead, he reconnected the dangerous fire, ripped off the sticker and warned his existing tenants that if they tried to warn the new tenants, he'd deduct their entire deposits.

Words *fail* me that I'm still hearing stories like this in the second millennium and after all that legislation.

Always keep records

Landlords should keep copies of old Gas Safety Certificates for at least five years to be on the safe side.

Make sure that your tenants never touch or try repairing gas appliances. To make sure this doesn't happen, inform your tenants that any issues to do with gas appliances (for example, repairs) must be reported to you *immediately*. Tenants must know where the cut off lever is situated and should contact Transco immediately if they smell gas – even if they can't contact their landlord.

Note: the Gas Service with 3★ cover is *not* a substitute for a Gas Safety Certificate – which is a specific range of safety tests, and requires a separate order and fee.

Carbon monoxide

Carbon monoxide is widely known as the silent killer and it doesn't only affect gas. Anything that burns can produce carbon monoxide. It's caused by the incomplete combustion of a variety of fuels – including coal fires. If you're the slightest bit concerned about your unit's facilities, *switch off* and call in a registered/accredited installer.

Many landlords (and householders) have a cheap yet effective carbon monoxide monitor in rooms where gas appliances are used.

Some newer restrictions

January 1996 saw the introduction of further restrictions particularly on gas appliances in bathrooms and bedrooms. Appliances used in these rooms must be of the room sealed type (check with your local Corgi installer). Some exceptions can be made for non-room sealed heaters but only if they have automatic cut-off devices (but again – check with your local Corgi installer).

In October 1998 the installation of instant water heaters (the old geysers) which don't have automatic cut out devices and which aren't the room-sealed type were made illegal. Installation of any appliances *must be* completed by an authorised Corgi installer.

The penalties

Landlords who flout these gas safety requirements do so at their – to say nothing of their tenants' – peril.

Lives are at stake and, because the legislation is clear-cut – so are the penalties. Which include:

■ A criminal conviction.

■ The invalidation of your property insurance.

■ Unlimited fines.

■ Civil cases for damages.

■ Prison.

Electrical safety

Electrical safety is governed by the Electrical Equipment (Safety) Regulations 1994.

Unfortunately, safety matters are not so clear cut with electricity; unless offering large shared houses where the House in Multiple Occupation (HMO) specific regulations come into play – along with very specific electrical qualifications. For HMO information, read Lesson 13: Houses in multiple occupation – new rules for sharers.

However, for the majority of landlords with one or two tenants, the law on electrical safety is not so prescriptive. At present, the guidelines ask for an inspection by a certified electrician at least every five years. This is likely to change for many landlords who will now find themselves within the scope of environmental health officers since the new classifications of shared housing came into force in April 2006 (see Lesson 13).

Wise landlords have, at the very least, a certified electrician examine any building before letting out to tenants. Landlords should undertake a check-up between tenancies for general issues and arrange for a qualified electrician to test the circuits at least every two years.

Note: by landlord check-ups I mean between every tenancy. Tenants can be surprisingly heavy handed with electrical sockets – many come loose and need securing regularly.

The contact breaker
A contact breaker system is an invaluable boon for private landlords. Once installed, it will simply fuse the circuit if tenants bring along a faulty iron or hairdryer – and it's *so* much cheaper than the average excess on a fire claim. Landlords need to assess their responsibilities under 'due diligence' in common law.

Carry out regular checks on electrical circuits
Ask a qualified certified electrician to check out your services regularly and keep the receipt for this check. Landlords running HMOs are currently required to have a landlord's electrical check annually by an NICEIC accredited electrician who will supply you with the appropriate certification.

■ Ensure that earth tags are in place.

■ Ensure that sockets comply with current regulations and are securely fixed to walls.

■ Make sure that your tenant knows where the main fuse box is for emergencies and how to use the fuse box/contact breakers.

■ Ensure that tenants telephone you or your agent *as soon as* an electrical fault develops.

■ Make certain that repairs are carried out immediately – tenants may be tempted to use faulty sockets etc if they have no alternative and you could find yourself liable for accidents.

Provide adequate, safe, space heating for your unit

Tenants won't shiver if the central heating is inadequate – they'll buy a cheap fire and plug it in. This is a dangerous situation, one that could damage your property, injure tenants or even cause fires. One landlord I know is rebuilding an entire property because tenants dried their clothes on storage heaters once too often, went out and managed to burn down the building.

Smoke Detectors Act 1991

Buildings built after 1992 must have smoke detectors on every floor. This is the legal position. But responsible landlords put smoke detectors in halls and kitchens of every rental unit – no matter what age they are.

Heat detectors

Heat detectors can be legal requirements in HMOs and the scope of these HMOs may be about to widen as the 2004 Act beds in. Be aware that fire detection in all its forms is an investment not a penalty.

Fire doors

Often a legal requirement in HMOs, fire doors are a sensible idea for landlords of all persuasions on means of escape. Your local fire officer will advise you – fire doors usually offer a half-hour fire resistance, an intumescent strip, which, when exposed to heat expands to contain smoke – and a permanently sprung 'self-closer' which makes sure that fire doors always spring closed. Landlords who need to install any or all of these measures to comply with HMO regulations should avoid cheap self-closers. They tend to bang rather than glide shut and cause endless tenant-to-tenant rows – another management issue you can live without.

Fire extinguishers and blankets

Every landlord needs to protect their building and tenants with these basic facilities. In larger, multiply-occupied buildings, environmental health officers will specify large fire extinguishers, usually located on the means of escape. Landlords often rent these from a large company, who service them regularly. On a smaller scale, all rentals would benefit from a domestic sized extinguisher which is located in kitchens. Available from any DIY store, they often come with a wall fixing (which I personally discard as removing the extinguisher can be very awkward). They cost just over £10. Fire blankets are another cheap but useful tool – again, they cost around £10.

The 1992 Building Regulations

These Regulations have, in new build and extensions to properties, increased attention to safety considerably. But landlords with old buildings can't just claim that they didn't know. You're in business and are *expected* to know.

Glass safety

Glass safety isn't covered specifically in rentals (except where you need to replace glass). But landlords need to make sure that the glass in French windows, in doors of any type – and in any vulnerable point in the building is toughened or safety, whichever applies. Any landlord with queries should contact their local environmental health officer for advice.

Lead pipes/water supplies

All landlords should ensure that old-fashioned lead water pipes are replaced with copper or a modern plastic system. It's the responsible thing to do with such a long-term investment.

Anything else?

As a landlord, you remain responsible for everything that you provide within the building – and legally liable. Tenants are now protected under consumer legislation, by health and safety and by Trading Standards – as well as the usual common law available to anyone – quite simply because action was needed to cut the death and accident rate in rented accommodation which has been historically dangerous.

Floors in kitchens and bathrooms should be non-slip. Latches and catches need to operate smoothly. Cookers shouldn't be installed right next to kitchen doors (making it impossible to escape).

There's only one rule – if you supply it, make sure it's safe.

Modern tenants are also entitled to take civil actions for damage and injury – and with the explosion of no-win no-fee – it's getting easier and easier to sue your landlord.

Take stock for general safety. Look inside the building and then beyond to the pathways and garden. Check that things are secure and that pathways don't become slippery. Anything which overhangs should be checked to make sure it is safe and cannot fall down (eg loose slates).

Don't let this put you off

You're expected to take reasonable care, not (despite what some of the landlord websites claim) to wrap tenants in bubble wrap – nor can you protect them from their own actions, or be responsible for freakish accidents. Nor can you be held liable for dangerous items that tenants bring into your unit without your knowledge.

How to check the building during a tenancy

And, finally, any halfway decent lease reserves any landlord's right to enter the property with 24 hours' written advance notice, which more than covers things like gas safety and a regular safety/ maintenance audit.

Whys and wherefores

This short lesson shouldn't take long to read through. Contact your local authority and ask for Trading Standards if you require any further help. Beyond that, provide the basic safe furniture, keep the services safe, and get your landlord's Gas Safety Certificate.

This particular section doesn't require a checklist/summary as each short section is easy to follow.

Lesson 13

Houses in Multiple Occupation

The old rules

There have been rules governing shared housing, multiply-occupied premises, bedsits, elderly conversions and buildings that ran over three or more floors that all local authorities could enforce since the enactment of the Housing Act 1985. What we are discussing in this lesson is *new legislation*. The Housing Act 2004 came into force in April 2006 and represent a significant change to the way in which landlords and agents let out property to all sharers.

What is a House in Multiple Occupation (HMO) under the old rules?

Under section 345 of the Housing Act 1985, it used to be defined as 'a house which is occupied by persons who do not form a single household'. Up and down the country, local environmental health officers used this definition to ensure that buildings occupied by a variety of tenants were safe. Buildings classified as HMOs under the old legislation were usually those with five or more sharers, bedsits, old conversions, etc. The reason for the legislation was simple. Five separate meals being cooked equals five times the fire risk. These rules covered a variety of scenarios – from single-bedroomed flats in elderly conversions; hostels where many people shared amenities; right through to large, complex house shares. In other words, a minority of landlords running very particular types of units were affected.

Why the law was changed recently

Unfortunately, at a time when the numbers of young people leaving home to attend university exploded, a landmark legal judgement (*Barnes v Sheffield City Council (1995) 27 HLR 719*) moved the goalposts. Previously, local authorities only intervened when they felt that student accommodation was clearly inadequate. Environmental health departments did not have the resources to harass every landlord in town. Nor were they interested in penalising responsible student landlords – only those trying to maximise profit at the potential cost of someone else's safety.

Unfortunately, this landmark legal judgement decreed that – under the Housing Act 1985 – students sharing houses could effectively be legally regarded as a single household. This, in effect, meant that most student housing (despite often being some of the worst) was exempt from the protection of environmental health officers and that safety measures on clearly unsatisfactory housing could not be enforced, where students had all signed a single lease.

What is both interesting and already being mis-reported is that local authorities already had powers to enforce safety on almost all of the 2004 Act's 'compulsory' section. Most problem units have already been tackled and standards have risen exponentially.

What was certainly *not* required to solve these issues was a five-year consultation and legislative proposal to protect tenants in property that was *already* largely protected by the 1985 Act. The reason for this extended process was driven by the *Barnes v Sheffield City Council* case and the outcome clearly allows local authorities across England and Wales to intervene much more extensively than was envisaged by the 1985 Acts.

Defining a 'single household' as one person – a co-habiting couple – or a single family – as they now have, is a very radical move.

Thus, many more landlords will now be running units which are HMOs – though many will still not require a licence – yet.

Some local authorities will use their new discretionary powers to licence some smaller shared units almost immediately, as it's now a local choice.

Others will act more slowly or discriminately. This is likely to vary significantly – area by area. Why? Because each borough contains massively different types, styles and age of property. Where older, shoddy housing is used en masse to house tenants (particularly the young and the poor) a local authority is likely to be very concerned. In newer towns, where the student population, for example, is housed in pretty reasonable accommodation, their concern is likely to be less.

Any landlord whose property falls into the compulsory section must contact their local authority *immediately*. Other landlords whose property falls into the discretionary sections of the legislation will need to keep a careful eye on their individual local authority's policy – both now and in the future – as this legislation is likely to 'evolve'. However, over time, local authorities may decide to impose policies over a far wider range that at present. Their opportunity to do so is very clear to anyone reading through the licensing section on the Department of Communities and Local Government website. This could mean that many thousands of landlords with modest tenant numbers of two or three could find themselves running HMOs. This is particularly clear from the short question and answer section later in this Lesson between myself and the ODPM in February 2006.

The role of environmental health officers

Theirs is a necessary and often thankless task. However, investors should understand that we cannot take 50 per cent of a tenant's income each week and expect to be allowed to get away with dangerous conditions. Environmental health officers do a vital job in protecting *our* young people, and *our* more vulnerable adults. So, no one is trying to put you out of business. However, standards that may cost some money to implement may well be required, now or soon.

WARNING ANECDOTE

Flushed with success over *Barnes v Sheffield City Council*, up and down the country, landlords and agents tried endless testing of the boundaries of what could and could not be safety regulated. Barnes had claimed that his students 'lived as a single family unit' – and would 'look out for one another in emergencies'. This was accepted (though plenty of us with kids of university age might wonder). Nevertheless, a legal judgement had been made. Student sharers were exempt.

Next came endless pressure to relax safety in *all shared housing* culminating with a test case between Islington Council and one of its landlords. Despite owning a huge house let out to nine individuals on separate leases – who all had their own lockable rooms and who, as total strangers, merely shared bathrooms and kitchens, this landlord claimed that his tenants also lived as a single 'unit' because they had a rota for cleaning the common hallway. Though students had proved an exception under the 1985 Act, other sharers were more fortunate. This landlord lost.

The 2004 legislation (in operation from April 2006) makes potential provision for almost *all* shared properties to be licensed – and puts all landlords who rely on more than one tenant to pay the rent on imminent notice of change.

New rules from April 2006

This guide attempts to escort you down the widest of the new legislative avenues but *any* landlord who rents property to any combination of rent payers needs to contact their local environmental health officers *now* for detailed guidance. This lesson is *no* substitute for the detailed technical help you will need to comply with these complex new laws if you rent out shared property. Landlords need to check for future policy changes – where councils can make charges, they tend to act – and licenses are already being mooted at costs ranging between £100 and £1,000.

The new definition of a 'household'

The new definition encompasses:

- A family.
- Single persons.
- Co-habiting couples (whether or not of the opposite sex).

Though still in its infancy, the old idea of shared housing has undergone a radical adjustment – strengthening by a considerable amount any council's enthusiasm for knowing what's going on inside those investments of yours.

Any sharing (with that exception of co-habiting couples or genuine families) means that the property is an HMO – no matter how the lease is organised. How your own local authority decides to interpret its new powers is crucial. And this definition is so narrow that tens of thousands of landlords may, wholly unwittingly, find themselves being caught up in the HMO net. The status of tenants becomes immaterial – this new regime is a simple numeric equation. Three City lawyers in a smart flat equals an HMO (though the council may or may not demand licences). Far more detailed information is available as usual at: *www.communities.gov.uk*. Click the 'licensing' or 'HMO' links.

Exceptions to the new legislation

- Buildings or parts of buildings, occupied by no more than two households each of which comprises a single person (ie a two-person flat share).
- Buildings occupied by a resident landlord with up to two tenants.
- Buildings managed or owned by a public body (such as the police or NHS) or a local housing authority or a registered social landlord.
- Where the residential accommodation is ancillary to the principle use of the building, eg religious establishments, conference centres, etc.
- Student halls of residence, where the education establishment has an Approved Code of Practice.
- Buildings regulated otherwise than under the Housing Acts such as care homes, bail hostels, etc and the description of which are specified in regulations.
- Buildings entirely occupied by freeholders or long leaseholders.

However, for those of you who just felt a chill down their spine, I defy you, having read the fascinating replies from the ODPM to my queries, to believe that this is anything less than a sea change for a huge number of us. The Q&A took place prior to the legislation coming into force.

Q **What happens if a two-bedroom flat – let by the landlord/ agent to two single, non-related persons – is sublet by the tenant to one additional person without the management's knowledge or consent – will this unit still be an HMO?**

A Yes it will be an HMO – in your tenancy agreement you should make it clear that tenants cannot sub-let.

Q **If this happens and the landlord/agent is served with a notice to comply with the HMO regulations, who will be liable for the cost of remedial works to bring the building into statutory compliance, if the tenant has broken a condition of their lease by sub-letting?**

A Landlord/agent.

Q **How is the management (landlord/agent) supposed to be able to prevent or supervise this – without breaching a tenant's right to 'quiet enjoyment'?**

A In the tenancy agreement, it should be made clear that tenants should not sub-let, the landlord/agent should also know who is renting the property at the start of the tenancy agreement and *throughout the life of the tenancy agreement* (emphasis added). Landlords/agents should also make regular checks of the property.

Q **If the tenant sub-lets and charges no rent – is an HMO still created?**

A Yes – if the property is sub-let making it suitable for operating as an HMO, it will need a licence.

Q **Will service of a Notice to Quit on tenants who have created an HMO without their management's knowledge or consent be sufficient to suspend any notification demanding HMO improvements?**

A Again, it depends on the property being suitable for operating as an HMO and whether it is going to be used as an HMO. If it is going to be rented out and operated as an HMO then it will need to have a licence. If this is an issue you have with your property, you may want to check with your local authority as they may want to see some sort of proof that the property will not be let out as an HMO.

Q Will landlords be legally obliged to understand that they are operating an HMO – or not?

A Yes, all landlords requiring HMO licences will be required to apply for a licence from 6 April 2006. There will be a grace period of three months to allow landlords sufficient time to send in applications once the three month period is up, any landlords requiring a licence who have not applied will be subject to legal proceedings, ie fines.

Q Will landlords who have no awareness that this new legislation affects them (the thousands of small portfolio landlords operating one/two/three bedroom properties without letting agents or membership of any landlord association) – who breach this legislation through complete ignorance of its existence – still be liable for a fine of up to £20,000 – or does this only apply if a 'licence' is breached? If so, what sanctions will be placed on landlords who don't *know* their obligations and fall foul of the law?

A The ODPM will be running a national publicity campaign. By 6 April [2006] all landlords should be aware of the requirement to have a licence. Once licensing becomes law in April 2006 there will be a three-month grace period in which landlords will be encouraged to apply for a licence without becoming liable for fines. If landlords who have not applied for a licence after this three-month grace period and are found to be operating an HMO illegally, they will face fines of up to £20,000.

Q Is there a précis (shortened version) of the new Hazard Rating System for landlords – the full guidelines are 193 pages long and far too technical for a layman?

A There is a factsheet on the HHSRS system. The address is: *www.odpm.gov.uk/hmo*.

Q **Does this new legislation supersede the** *Barnes v Sheffield City Council* **case, which managed to exempt student sharers on a single lease?**

A Yes. It will supersede *Barnes v Sheffield City Council*. Here is more detail.

i. A single household is defined by section 258 of the Housing Act 2004.

ii. A house shared by unrelated students is an HMO (unless it is a building exempted by Schedule 14 of the 2004 Act).

iii. If the house is occupied by five or more persons (who form two or more households) and is of more than three storeys, it is subject to mandatory licensing.

iv. If the house is smaller/and occupied by fewer persons, it is still an HMO, subject to certain statutory controls but the local housing authority has discretion as to whether to make a licensing scheme that would cover such properties.

Unanswered queries

Here are two final questions that getting answers to has not been possible.

1. What happens to a unit that slides in and out of the licensing requirements as sometimes it's let out to two, other times to three – depending on the market conditions?

2. Once licensed, what precisely do you have to do to become unlicensed? Or will that building be licensed for a period of time that may affect its saleability on the open market?

Still confused?

Small wonder. After all these years of consultation, we still don't have the one thing we needed, a national standard that all local authorities and landlords are forced to adhere to and applied across the board so we all knew exactly where we stood and our costs matched our local competitors. This 'will they? won't they?' is a nightmare for those crunching tight numbers. The vast majority of rentals involve more than one tenant – and each local authority will *still* be able to decide for itself which buildings may require a licence and which may not.

What do these new laws mean I need to do?

Any landlord who rents out property that clearly offers accommodation to *more than one of the legally defined households*, needs to discuss matters with their local environmental health department. Just make your call. Environmental health officers are not the private landlord's enemy, they exist to raise standards in what is often pretty poor accommodation. Remember, they often see the worst, rarely the best – and this is bound to affect their view of our industry. But most EHOs are helpful goldmines of information. They don't want to penalise you – but they have legal responsibilities to enforce safety and they just became a whole lot more important to most landlords in the UK.

Will I need a licence?

Many landlords who rent out everything from swanky mansion flats in the City to two bed-room terraces in the north are going to find themselves on the local authorities' radar. A good rule of thumb is that every landlord who relies on more than one income to pay rent needs to contact their local authority promptly and enquire whether or not that type of housing in their area has been locally designated as requiring a licence to operate yet. If so, you need to apply and comply. No debate.

What happens if I don't report that I'm letting out an HMO?

As you read in my Q&A, landlords who ought to have a licence and fail to apply will be fined. Although your local authority may decide that you don't need a licence to operate, you'd have to have very deep pockets to *assume* that much when £20,000 fines are being bandied about. Plus, read the last paragraph of this Lesson – for a true toe-curling moment. These laws have teeth and they will bite unwary or under-informed landlords.

What can the local authority make me do to the building to obtain a licence?

More muddy water I'm afraid. Where local authorities used to be able to have a uniform set of standards (a certain type of wiring standard, fire doors, so many electrical sockets per room, etc), the new 2004 Act introduces a mouthful of letters – the HHSRS (Housing Health and Safety Rating System) with its 193 pages of endlessly interpretable guidelines. Each unit applying for a license needs to be separately assessed and hazards 'rated' by environmental health officers against a Byzantine formula.

Yet again, I can see the logic. Given the sheer numbers of properties that may eventually fall into a licensed category, it does seem mad to insist that (say) a nearly new three-bedroomed house on a smart estate (as opposed to the shabby old terraced house with exactly the same number of tenants sharing) has to have all its wiring replaced etc. But this complexity makes it very difficult for investors to know exactly what is required.

Rather than a clear set of rules, environmental health officers are required to make professional assessments based on a new safety rating system. I can see endless challenges as one State EHO makes one professional assessment – only to be challenged by an equally qualified and professional Private EHO engaged by a landlord, who makes a different, equally professional assessment.

Here we are back in Whitehall's beloved land of unintended consequence. When *will* they learn?

But these new rules won't affect me ... will they?

As for those landlords and agents, currently so certain that these new rules won't affect them, I'm afraid I don't share their confidence. Local authorities have been running Registration Schemes and piloting licences for years. They know their own areas well and they've had (rightly in my view) powers to serve improvement notices on larger buildings and larger house shares since 1985 – and have done a good job in raising standards. The reason behind this new legislation was to correct the *Barnes v Sheffield City Council* anomaly – in other words, they've already tackled the most dangerous housing scenarios – this legislation is designed to bring smaller scale operations under their safety umbrella. For those of you tearing your hair out by the roots, let me assure you that your three-bedroom semi housing three students may well be pristine. Unfortunately, across the country, many are appalling and, due to the *Barnes v Sheffield City Council* judgement, so long as four or less students signed a single lease, there wasn't a thing the local authority could do to protect those tenants – until now.

Why has the bar about what constitutes an HMO been set so low?

I have no idea. Nor do I know anyone who expected a bar below 2 or 3. There will undoubtedly be legal challenges. The next three years promise to be yet more of those 'interesting times' the UK is so often in.

A breakdown of the main changes

■ HMO stands for House in Multiple Occupation.

■ A single household consists of one family, one co-habiting couple or a singleton.

■ The 2004 Act makes it compulsory to license larger, high risk rentals.

■ The 2004 Act *allows* councils to run licensing schemes on smaller shared properties.

■ The 2004 Act creates three types of license:

1. *Compulsory*
   For properties that are three or more storeys high; have five or more tenants who share amenities such as bathrooms/kitchens.

2. *Additional licensing of HMOs*
   Discretionary powers that councils may decide to apply to a particular type of HMO – for example, students or asylum seekers (or any others it considers a priority).

3. *Selective licensing (mainly discussed in this lesson)*
   Properties that are not subject to mandatory HMO licensing could be also be covered under a selective licensing scheme. This is where the local authority may declare certain areas (eg where there is low demand or anti-social behaviour) as appropriate for selective licensing. This could cover many forms of rented property including a vast number of shared arrangements.

Collectively – these three forms of licensing potentially cover virtually every type and income bracket of property across the UK.

To obtain a license

Anyone who owns or manages a compulsory HMO (unless your borough has decided to classify other types of sharing immediately) that must be licensed has to apply to the local authority for a licence. The local authority should give a licence if satisfied that:

1. The HMO is suitable for the number of people allowed under the licence.
2. The proposed licence holder is a fit and proper person.
3. The proposed management arrangements are satisfactory.
4. The financial structures of the management are suitable.
5. That fees are paid.

How long will a licence last?

A maximum of five years.

Can I be refused a licence?

Yes – unless you comply with the requirements made on the number of occupants, condition of building, facilities and contents.

Can I operate without one?

No – not unless you fancy the fine.

Can I appeal if they refuse me a license?

You must appeal to the Residential Property Tribunal (details available through the local authority) within 28 days of being refused a licence.

You mentioned fines – are there any other sanctions?

A £20,000 fine for not having a licence – and £5,000 if you breach any licence conditions.

Oh, and just one final sanction

Tenants living and paying rent in accommodation that should have been licensed – but wasn't – can claim back all the rent they paid during the unlicensed period (up to 12 months' worth of it.). They also need to approach the Residential Property Tribunal to lodge a complaint. Councils can reclaim housing benefit they paid out too.

Whys and wherefores

As usual, the best sources of information on this topic remain the government on *www.communities.gov.uk*. Look for Housing in Multiple Occupation, or licensing links and click through what you find – looking for factsheets. The Royal Institute of Chartered Surveyors' website is another good one to try on: *www.rics.co.uk*. All environmental health departments have had additional training provided by the government. to help prepare them for the changes so you can telephone for informed advice.

CHECKLIST/SUMMARY

- The new legislation came into force from April 2006.

- All landlords who let property to more than one tenant need to contact their environmental health department to check what the local interpretation of these laws will be.

- Local authorities have been given sweeping powers that have the potential to regulate most landlords.

- Some properties will require immediate licensing – check.

- This new legislation is a simple numeric calculation – three tenants in one unit always equals an HMO. Two tenants in some limited cases could also be an HMO.

- Licensing of HMOs, however, is far from automatic – each local authority will decide for itself how to interpret these vast new categories of housing according to local conditions.

- The government has introduced a Byzantine Hazard Safety scheme for all HMOs (HHSRS). There is a factsheet on this topic on the government website. Although 193 pages long, the details so far don't include fire prevention measures.

- Landlords with questions should email: *licensing@communities. gov.uk*.

- Local authorities will only issue licences where they feel it is appropriate – in terms of the building and amenities. This may also mean that some landlords will need to reduce tenant numbers to comply.

- Landlords wishing to operate outside the scope of licensing altogether will need to have very low tenant numbers indeed.

- Licences can be refused. There is an appeal procedure.

Lesson 14

Property maintenance

The problem with property maintenance is two-fold. It costs a good deal – and spending only gets you back to where you started.

Obtaining consents

Don't forget – before you buy any property that needs work, that the smallest of alterations (like chimney breast removal) can need local authority approvals. All new and replacement windows need to comply with strict new regulations which are rigorously enforced. Landlords are not the most popular of neighbours. Someone will report you. Then you'll have the double trouble of ripping out the inadequate work and starting over again.

Initial purchases are fraught with issues, simply to make them suitable for tenants. That leaky bath seal might be fine for a careful family, but tenants *won't* take care. You'll end up with staining (or worse) on the downstairs ceiling. And insurance policies are for accidental damage, not to save your maintenance budget.

Anyone buying a rental property needs to learn to be realistic. Make rentals *durable*.

It's always tempting to do things as cheaply as possible. We all try it once. But experience teaches landlords the value of foresight. Look at your building realistically. If you choose to have the whole place skimmed (plastered) that may well be a long-term investment in the building. In the vast majority of rentals, tenants won't pay any more money for pristine plasterwork than they will for lined walls emulsioned the same colour.

Floor stripping can be an excellent idea – except where noise is an issue and never on stairways. Tenants love stripped wood floors. They like less the cost of re-sanding and re-coating them when their friends came round wearing steel-tipped shoes.

The building

Rental property needs to be in reasonable condition and to be kept in reasonable condition. Otherwise the calibre of the tenants will fall away – along with rent levels. Tenants are increasingly sophisticated. They aren't usually looking for the moon, but they do expect something decent in return for half their income. Shabby looking buildings simply don't rent as easily as well maintained ones. Saving a few hundred pounds on the paintwork and fences is a false economy.

Freehold buildings

Liability for all repairs and maintenance

Landlords need to take maintenance seriously. All landlords should set aside between six and ten per cent of all the rent they receive for maintenance. It sounds like a lot – but in reality, that's barely enough to build a sinking fund for new boilers, internal and external decorating and the odd roof repair.

Because here's the thing. Well cared for buildings take hardly any management time. The boiler shouldn't always be playing up. The roof shouldn't leak. The toilet shouldn't block or sinks overflow. Knowing that you handed over everything in good working order makes it easier to know whether it's the building or tenant causing problems.

Roof

The roof must be watertight. It's a management nightmare dealing with roof leaks in bleak Januarys which invariably cost more. Emergency repairs *are always* more expensive than routine maintenance.

Chimney

Chimneys must be in decent condition – pots fall if not maintained – and they can cause immense damage. Old flashings can deteriorate and allow water penetration. Let property is a stitch-in-time kind of business.

Windows

Windows must work and have easy to operate mechanisms – tenants won't take the kind of care required to limp a rotten window frame through the winter. Plastic windows might be maintenance-free but slash the resale value of older buildings. French windows, glazed doors, etc must be safe and fitted with the appropriate glass. Tenants will hold you liable if they open up a well-loved artery as their hand goes through the front door because you hadn't ensured that the glass was toughened/safety type glazing. Exterior paintwork should be done every three to five years and many buildings require the extra expense of scaffolding.

Bricks

Brick built buildings do require infrequent (but costly) re-pointing. This keeps the building watertight – otherwise expect problems with damp and damaged interior finishes. And cut back that ivy. It can penetrate and take water with it.

Stucco

Most stucco work requires specialists to repair. Badly maintained, it can blister and fall with a gentle thump onto pavements (and heads). Don't do it yourself – all you'll achieve is a devaluation of the property.

Guttering

Make regular checks on rainwater goods and guttering. Most need an annual clear out as they fill with autumn leaves. This needn't be an expensive job – most window cleaners will happily do this for a small charge – but it is an essential one. Congested guttering results in overflowing which causes long-term damage to the building. And this is an investment, remember?

Wastes/plumbing

Water pipes – the bane of every landlord's life. Obviously, the main soil stacks are exterior and, in many cases, still cast iron. Check them for leaks on a fairly regular basis. If they begin to deteriorate, have them replaced properly. And find yourself a decent plumber.

Plumbing

Interior plumbing should not be lead – environmental health will have a fit! And it must work well. Hot and cold water is a vital facility. Problems with these should be an emergency status for landlords. Same-day repairs (or within 48 hours as an absolute maximum) is essential.

Bathrooms

Power showers are not essentials in anything but the highest specification units. In fact, they are a well-known industry problem. A standard showerhead connected to a good source of hot water is perfectly adequate.

Make sure that all water is well contained. Seals and gaskets must be top notch – and floor coverings in kitchens and bathrooms really do need to be waterproof/slip-proof.

Wiring

Wiring must be safe. Get any new purchases checked over by a well-qualified electrician and certified as safe. If you use the NICEIC and they're happy with the installation, they'll provide a Landlord's Certificate. Make sure that an electrician makes regular (say every two years) checks on the supply. And install a circuit breaker.

Tenants need a reasonable number of electrical sockets per room. Not providing what people are likely to need doesn't mean tenants won't use their TV/VCR, while simultaneously surfing the internet and printing documents, it means instead that your investment will be a spaghetti-like tangle of dangerous extensions and multi-plug adaptors.

Heating systems

Heating systems must work well and be safe. Gas systems must have current Gas Safety Certificates and it's a reasonable precaution to buy a carbon monoxide detector. In Central London (and presumably elsewhere) some areas have real trouble with mains water pressure – especially above the ground floor. This should be checked out *before* installing a modern combi-boiler system. Landlords should be wary about individual space heating, which can be precarious.

Kitchens

Kitchens need adequate food preparation surfaces, tiled splash backs, a decent fridge, a cooker, plus hot and cold water. Make sure there's a smoke alarm, a small fire extinguisher and a fire blanket as minimum fire safety standards. Those facilities can be placed within a very modest arrangement from any DIY store to a granite topped cherry wood masterpiece. What I would positively avoid are wooden work-tops – of whatever quality. They are far too high maintenance for the average tenant. Who wants to rent a flat then spend their evenings oiling wood?

Decorating

Keep it simple. Easy maintenance emulsioned walls are undoubtedly ideal. Always keep enough spare paint so that you can touch up between tenancies without redecorating the entire room.

Outside

Yet again, if there is an outside area, keep things simple. Tenants don't like gardening. Charge enough rent to cover garden maintenance and forget about it.

Leasehold buildings

Where landlords have long leases, pay ground rent and service charges

Flats have to be leasehold/shared freehold to work. This means that landlords have to worry less about the overall condition of the building itself as – theoretically - a management company somewhere will be organising all this for you. As a leaseholder, you're not only not responsible for the structure, you're positively discouraged from impacting on it.

Service charges are pricey – and often don't include major works at all. If the management decides that a new roof is required, it will divide the cost between the units and issue a bill to each of its leaseholders.

Whys and wherefores

I've deliberately kept this lesson short. It's one of the few topics that you will find a great deal of advice about. Your building has a two-fold income stream. One is the rent. Two is the ultimate sale price. How you decide to juggle each is one of the benefits of being your own boss. You'll find the Royal Institute of Chartered Surveyors' website valuable on this topic: *www.rics.co.uk*. They sometimes have free factsheets on building maintenance to order online. Be wary of taking advice on costly finishes from agents – it's not their money being spent. Alternatively, you may decide to do the bare minimum to the building and rent as is. It's another of those judgement calls you can make for yourself. Whichever way you decide to go, the advice given here is a minimum to protect your investment and your tenants, which together, constitute your precious income stream. Not looking after either is a mistake – and often downright illegal.

This lesson is so straightforward I haven't included a summary.

Lesson 15

The tax man's take

Tax. That iniquitous entity that some people spend all their lives trying to avoid. But like it or not, tax is part of every landlord's planning. And this is the shortest lesson of all. I've no intention of giving specialist advice in a guidebook. What landlords need are:

1. A qualified accountant to guide them through the maze of allowances, taxation vehicles and circumstances that best suit them.

2. A rough idea of what the tax man wants before they buy.

So, in answer to part two (you'll need to find an accountant of your own, all landlords need one), first, I'd like to make you smile. Having read this guide, you'll be astonished to learn that rental income is classified by the tax man as 'unearned income'. That's right – unearned. And that's, I'm afraid, the only smile you're likely to get from this lesson.

Landlords need specific advice, simply because everyone's financial circumstances differ so wildly. Some landlords pay basic rate tax – others are way into the higher tax brackets. Some will be better advised to operate on a simple sole trader basis – others would be well advised to use a small company trading basis. Beyond that, depending on how much you're willing to pay, the right combination of lawyer and accountant can stuff your rental income into a wide variety of taxation vehicles and strategies too numerous and complex to imagine.

For my money and peace of mind, I've always believed that I wasn't anything like wealthy enough to become involved with these shenanigans. Trying to evade tax for the average landlord is a mug's game. Tax is a fact of life for those not rich enough to evade it. And (though the unearned classification is a hang up from when only the truly rich were landlords and lived lives of Riley), the tax regime for most private landlords isn't that bad. Taxes are charged on 'net' income – ie the money left after all your deductible expenses have been taken off. Landlords find VAT difficult to recover if they operate as sole traders. And UK residents living abroad are still liable to pay income tax on UK generated rents.

Tax on income

Most things that are legitimate costs are tax deductible.

- Mortgage interest costs (in many cases – but you need to check circumstances).
- Council tax (where applicable).
- Service charges (for leasehold properties).
- Any legal costs involved in running the business (ie eviction costs).
- Insurance.
- Advertising.
- Agency costs.
- Management costs.
- . All stationery costs, legal forms and legal costs incurred.
- A proportion of your telephone costs.
- Window cleaning/cleaning costs.
- Gardening costs.
- Any works required between tenancies that aren't the responsibility of tenants.
- Any repairs to the building (but not improvements – upgrades are deductible from the capital gain you'll be charged on rising asset values).
- Any repairs to the interior.
- And – of course, any courses, guides, etc.
- Plus – all landlords can opt to have a standard ten per cent tax deduction for wear and tear.

So, not so bad. Landlords need to keep every single receipt for every single item or job done on their units and submit them to their accountant at the end of the year for deduction. That way, you'll become the proud owner of an annual set of certified accounts, which are brilliant for re-sale to other landlords.

Tax on asset appreciation

If you felt like tackling the income side of things – good for you. If you decide to try your hand at calculating the capital gains tax (CGT) on property inflation, you'll need more than luck.

Capital gains tax is chargeable on all property sales except that of your own main residence. It's therefore a critical part of the overall return calculations on all let properties.

This is where all those old bills from way back when you first purchased the property come into their own. Landlords aren't allowed to claim income tax relief on the installation of improvements like central heating, extra bathrooms or extensions. This is also the time to throw all the purchase costs and fees into the allowances pot as they can usually be offset against the overall price that you sell for as part of your complex CGT calculation.

CGT is a punitive tax on all speculative gain – ie gain you did nothing to earn. Now it might seem a bit unfair, but frankly, property prices doubling every three years is nothing to do with the paint finish and everything to do with the overall performance of the economy. It's charged on the difference between what you paid for a building and what you ultimately sell the same building for and the rate that you pay depends on your annual net income. Given that most landlords have already enjoyed income tax relief on interest payments for mortgages, and most repairs and renewals, this cannot feature twice.

But a vastly complex set of tapers can come into play – depending on how long you've owned the building. And an indexation calculation can also be used to modify the impact of inflation in your 'gain'.

Every UK resident also has an annual capital gains tax allowance of several thousands of pounds. This is when the value of good initial advice really counts. Buy as a couple and each of you enjoy a capital gains allowance in any tax year. Spread sales of investment to maximise this allowance. And, for those of you who've held property for decades, CGT was introduced in the early 1980s and isn't chargeable on gains made before that time. Hence the complex calculation matrix needed.

If you're up for it, try getting this right on your own. However, be sure that the few hundred pounds saving is really worth it. Last month, friends of mine sold a property that – as novice landlords – they'd never taken advice over. The husband had inherited the building and it had been let for several years. But no one had thought to put the building into both their names – hence only one allowance was claimable. These allowances run into thousands of pounds. It was a considerable loss of ten times what it would have cost to take an hour's advice. Any accountant would have picked this up instantly. So, not much of a saving.

When it comes to the hands-on elements of running property, I'm the country's biggest advocate of going it alone. Independent landlords can often do a better job for themselves (and their tenants) than any agent. But when we get down to specialist areas like these, I'm as passionate an advocate of using as many insured professionals as you can get your hands on. Then try *understanding* them!

Whys and wherefores

Those of you feeling especially plucky and who want to save on accountants' fees would do well to contact HM Revenue & Customs and request a copy of their *Taxation of rents: A guide to property income* (free booklet number R2P3067). The Capital Taxes office also produces booklets on capital gain and the tapering arrangements for taxpayers acquiring asset appreciation, CGT1. Request both through your local tax office. Alternatively, go online, there's a wealth of great advice out there if you search it out from reputable sources.

— CHECKLIST/SUMMARY —

■ Accountants understand tax in a way that novices rarely can. Like their colleagues, solicitors and surveyors, they're professionally indemnified for error and invariably worth their fee.

■ The way in which you structure a purchase can have major tax implications throughout your ownership and can have huge effects on tax due on disposal. Make sure you take advice early, when it matters.

■ Items that are needed to run the unit are deductible from income tax.

■ Items that involve purchase and or improvement/investment costs are only deductible when you sell from CGT.

■ Everyone has a capital gains allowance each year – make sure that you use it wisely.

Index by Topic

The Serious Responsibilities

Houses in Multiple Occupation (HMOs)

Index